THE EAGLE
The Autobiography of Santa Anna

THE EAGLE

The Autobiography of Santa Anna

Edited by Ann Fears Crawford

1967 · THE PEMBERTON PRESS · AUSTIN

For "Tony"

Introduction

AS A MAKER OF HISTORY, General Antonio Lopez de Santa Anna is a controversial figure. There has been no tide of nostalgia rising up to obscure the details of his life. Instead, clouds of controversy continue to surround him, making it difficult to distinguish truth from legend. Too little is known of him to analyze fully the impact of his involvement in the political and military events which shaped the destiny of Mexico and North America.

This first publication in English of his handwritten autobiography should provide a fresh insight and a renewal of interest in the events which led to his political eclipse. His own expression of the burdens of a man forced to measure his own achievements has been criticized as an example of exaggeration and as evidence of a stubborn unwillingness to admit personal error on any level. This type of fatuous criticism, though certainly in some measure true, should decrease in the light of more information and mature historical investigation after the period of partisan emotions has finally passed. Never have a nation and its own historians been more shackled by these emotions than Mexico.

Each generation has its heroes; yet the legacy of the past continues to be a source of intrigue for every generation. It had long been the dream of General Santa Anna's grandson and namesake, Antonio Lopez de Santa Anna, S.J., to bridge the gap from one generation to another by bringing to light the personal vision of Santa Anna and the role he played in the history of Mexico, Texas, and the United States. This English translation was one of his dreams, and his recent death saddens those of us who knew and admired him all the more because he was unable to witness it.

Father Santa Anna entered the Jesuit order in 1897, at the age of sixteen, and became a priest in 1913. After twenty-six exemplary years of teaching in various colleges and universities in Europe, he volunteered for missionary work and was assigned to the primitive frontier between the Dominican Republic and Haiti. It was during this period that he began to appreciate the obstacles encountered by the General in his attempt to form a political community. He also recognized the parallel course of their two lives. Although the individual ends and means were distinctly different, Father Santa Anna was able to relate a unity of purpose and a familiarity with the past which were for him almost an extension of the life of his grandfather in another generation.

I first met Father Santa Anna in San Juan, Puerto Rico, after his retirement from the mission. Unlike his grandfather, his achievements in the Dominican Republic had been highly praised by others, especially by the citizens he had met on the raw frontier. Before his death, he kindly afforded me many interviews and often referred to his personal copy of General Santa Anna's *Memoirs* to elaborate various anecdotes about his grandfather. His own hopes of writing a definitive biography of his grandfather and of editing and annotating these *Memoirs* cannot now be accomplished, but the witness of his life and the interest he developed in others for such a project has been fulfilled. His wish that the General's *Memoirs* receive contemporary consideration has led to what I hope will be the beginning of a fresh evaluation of General Santa Anna and of his pivotal role in the history of three nations.

JAIME S. PLATÓN
San Juan, Puerto Rico
October, 1966

Preface

No MAN was more a reflection of his times and of his surroundings than Antonio Lopez de Santa Anna. He rose from the ranks of the Mexican army to serve eleven times as the chief executive of the Mexican nation. Not once did he serve in a legislative body; not once did he serve as a member of a Cabinet. His spectacular rise to power—and his fall from honor— are entirely in keeping with Mexico's turbulent history in an era of cruelty, dictatorship, and consistent upheaval.

Vain, egotistical, cocksure, he could have been no other kind of ruler but a dictator. Tales of his greed, his excesses with both women and drugs are tantamount to legends throughout Mexico and Texas. And yet, beneath the surface, there seems to abide the desire to serve his country, the desire to dedicate himself to his nation. This was the enigma of Santa Anna.

Fanny Calderon de la Barca, the witty and charming wife of Spain's first envoy to independent Mexico, presents perhaps the most penetrating portrait of

Santa Anna. She visited his estate, Manga de Clavo, in 1839, while the General was in retirement.

"In a little while entered General Santa Anna himself, a gentlemanly, good-looking, quietly-dressed, rather melancholy-looking person, with one leg, apparently a good deal of an invalid, and to us decidedly the best looking and most interesting figure in the group. He has a sallow complexion, fine dark eyes, soft and penetrating, and an interesting expression of face. Knowing nothing of his past history, one would have said a philosopher, living in dignified retirement—one who had tried the world and found that all was vanity, one who had suffered ingratitude and who, if he were ever persuaded to emerge from his retreat, would only do so, Cincinnatus-like, to benefit his country. It is strange, and a fact worthy of notice in natural history, how frequently this expression of philosophic resignation, of placid sadness, is to be remarked on the countenances of the most cunning, the deepest, most ambitious, most designing and most dangerous statesmen I have seen. [They have] a something that would persuade the multitude that they are above the world, and engage in its toils only to benefit others—so that one can hardly persuade oneself that these men are not saints . . . above all, witness the melancholy and philosophic Santa Anna.

". . . he was quiet and gentlemanly in his manners. Yet here sat with this *air de philosophe* perhaps one of the worst men in the world—ambitious of power—greedy of money —and unprincipled—having feathered his nest at the expense of the republic—and waiting in a dignified retreat only till the moment comes for putting himself at the head of another revolution."

Terrible as she may have found his actions, Fanny, must have found Santa Anna, the man, fascinating. So did many other women. The tales of his escapades with women are rivaled only by those of his great wealth. Many accounts detail the striking and sumptuous battle array he exhibited at San Jacinto. One account states, "Santa Anna, it is said, wore in his shirt three studs, valued at $1700 each; upon these was written his name, in parts, as follows: *Antonio— Lopez de—Santa Anna*. His camp furniture was exceedingly rich and splendid; he had silver tea urns, silver cream pots; splendid china ware, marked in monograms; rich cut glass tumblers and decanters, the latter with stoppers mounted with gold; and almost every thing compatible with a camp which could contribute to comfort and luxury." A silken tent, silken sheets, and silken underclothes helped, no doubt, to make the sultry Gulf Coast climate more comfortable for "El Presidente."

His "way with women" was legendary, and his illegitimate children lend credence to the legends. Although he considered himself quite a connoisseur of women, he undoubtedly chose poorly at least once. A certain Louisa, with quite a mercenary streak in her heart, became incensed when Santa Anna refused to give her money. After spending several nights at his palace, she stole away with all the medals from his coat. She gaily flitted through the slums, bestowing on one peon the Order of Guadalupe; on another, the Order of Charles the III; and on yet another, the Cross of Tampico. It must have chagrined the "Napoleon of the West" no end to have had to pay several thousand pesos more than the lady's original price to redeem his baubles.

The tales of his addiction to opium and to the sport of cock-fighting only added to the swaggering charms of the Hero of Tampico. To read his protests, his proclamations, his speeches is to discover a complete egotist, wallowing in the bombastic style he learned at the side of his hero, Carlos Maria Bustamente. But, as his devoted followers, the *Santanistas*, so often proclaimed, "Santa Anna, right or wrong! Santa Anna!"

Santa Anna's autobiography, the original manuscript of which is in The University of Texas Library, has been published only once before, in a small limited edition in Spanish, in 1906. An unpopular subject in Mexico, Santa Anna—by far the most colorful and historically important personage produced in Mexico during the past three hundred years—is unfortunately ignored and understandably passed over by native historians and political analysts. The neglect of this fascinating autobiography is but a case in point.

Many Americans, with the decided exception of that other egotist, Winfield Scott, found the "Napoleon of the West" fascinating. An attaché at the American Embassy during the height of Santa Anna's power wrote, "I have seen Santa Anna in his coach, surrounded with guards and all the pomp of the military, at the review of eight thousand troops; in church at prayer; in the ball room; in a cock-pit betting; in the audience room; at the banquet; and in private interviews of delicate diplomacy, when the political interests of the two nations were at stake. No one can easily forget him; according to public opinion he is a riddle in character; he surely is not in appearance; and if his person and his manners are not as with others to be taken as a fair index of the man, he is either an arch-hypocrite or a capital actor."

Anthony Butler, the United States Minister to Mexico in 1833, reflected on Santa Anna's character when he changed from a liberal outlook to a more conservative one. "For myself, I cannot think the event in the last doubtful, commence how and when they may—Gen. Santa Anna must prevail—everything favors him—He is in the first place an abler, and more of a practical man than can be found in the Ranks of his adversaries; He has the National resources at his command, and this would secure him the Majority of the Troops were there no other Consideration to operate—public sentiment (up to this period at least) is decidely in his favor . . .".

That Santa Anna believed he was the best ruler for Mexico cannot be doubted. His statements, his letters, and his *Memoirs* prove that he was convinced that he was just the "enlightened despot" his people needed. Another United States Minister, Joel R. Poinsett, once chastised Santa Anna for changing from his early liberal views. Santa Anna replied to him, ". . . it is very true that I threw up my cap for liberty with great ardor, and perfect sincerity, but very soon found the folly of it. A hundred years to come my people will not be fit for liberty. They do not know what it is, unenlightened as they are, and under the influence of a Catholic clergy, a despotism is the proper government for them, but there is no reason why it should not be a wise and virtuous one."

Perhaps if Santa Anna had hewn a course in his government that was more wise and more virtuous, his rule would have been a happier one—both for him and for the Mexican people. If this first translation of Santa Anna's *Memoirs* into English does no more than to reveal to us a little more about the man, it will have served its purpose.

In editing the *Memoirs* no attempt has been made to correct the many errors in the original manuscript. Notes following the text point out the more obvious errors. Santa Anna's memory, as he, himself, points out, certainly fails him on many occasions. We can only speculate that many of these failures were intentional. The fact that he began his *Memoirs* late in life and with the obvious intent of absolving himself for any blame in any situation accounts for many errors. Mistakes in names and places are corrected in brackets following the names that Santa Anna gives to the person or place.

Following the literal translation of Santa Anna's original manuscript, the only editing that has been done is to pull together the threads of his story and to make the events more readable through clarity. No additions or deletions have been made.

I wish to gratefully acknowledge the help of the translators, Sam Guyler and Jaime Platón. Special gratitude also goes to R. Henderson Shuffler, The Texana Program, The University of Texas, to the Honorable Ralph Yarborough, United States Senate, M. H. Loewenstern, and to Joada Hatton White for assistance in preparing the manuscript and the index.

General Santa Anna's grandson and namesake, Father Santa Anna III, had devoted many years of his life to a study of his grandfather's life and deeds. Father Santa Anna had agreed to write the Introduction to this volume, adding some of his own notes and personal recollections. Unfortunately, his untimely death has prevented his doing so. Father Santa Anna's own prospective biographer—for the Father led a remarkable life himself—Jaime Platón has kindly contributed an Introduction in his place.

Ann Fears Crawford
Austin, Texas
1 December 1966

Contents

xviii

xix

THE EAGLE
The Autobiography of Santa Anna

Prologue

IN THE HEARTS of most men there lurks a sentiment which they carefully try to hide from their fellow men. This foolish sentiment is that which causes man to aspire constantly to immortality. Not all men, however, succeed in inscribing their names on the walls of the temple of glory.

I cannot deny that when I was young the idea of glorifying my name passed through my mind. I aspired to perform noble deeds that would live forever in the hearts of men. In later years, however, a nobler sentiment, lacking all personal ambition, took its place and constantly directed all my actions. This sentiment was the love of liberty and the desire to glorify the name of my country. To this love of country which I have avowed, and to nothing else, I owe my transitory rise to power.

I desired to spend my life performing noble deeds for that magnificent country where I was born and reared. But the constant upheavals and surges of revolution opposed me. And, in their constant drive for power, not all the men who surrounded me could measure up to those aspirations of patriotism which motivated me.

Ostracized by my countrymen and in exile, I feel compelled to pick up my pen and write the true facts of my public life. Exiled from my country, I deplore the many errors of the men who have succeeded me in public office and the many misfortunes which have befallen my unhappy country. No desire for glory guides my unpracticed pen! My only desire is to leave to my fellow countrymen and to my heirs a faithful account of my public life. I wish to be judged by the truth, not by the tongues of antagonistic scoundrels.

In my long and worldly experience, I have discovered that a man in the public eye must suffer much. He suffers sometimes for the very gifts that nature endows him with, sometimes for his exalted services to his country, and sometimes merely for the fact that he is a celebrated personality. All people feel that they have the right to judge him at their own whim. They do judge him according to their whim, but they pass a quick and decisive sentence. Woe to the reputation of the public servant if poisonous slander touches it!

Happy, a thousand times happy, is he who lives his life unknown and dies tranquilly in his peaceful bed! How I have envied this unknown man throughout my life and how I envy him at this moment!

From the time I celebrated my first victories in the cause of my country's liberty to the time when the people first took me to their hearts, hatred and envy followed me. Blasphemy, sarcasm, slander—all followed me like a shadow. At each new triumph in my career, ill-feeling increased.

I, being young, inexperienced, and without a cloud on my conscience, occupied myself solely with helping Mexico become a nation. Nothing more! And I succeeded, without losing any Mexican territory. Seduced by the flattery of others during these days of glory, I allowed myself to be elevated to the office of President. Ah, then the disappointments, then the disillusions! Let it suffice to say, that I have been exiled from my beloved Mexico three times, this last exile lasting for more than eighteen years.

In conclusion, I must state that, as I have dedicated myself entirely to the noble profession of defending my country, these last *Memoirs* may be lacking in literary style. In reading these pages, the reader will soon discover that the author is a soldier, not a writer. Nevertheless, truth will not be lacking! I leave it to my readers, in their infinite wisdom, to judge my character and deeds without prejudice. I will abide by their sentence.

General Antonio Lopez de Santa Anna
Nassau in the Bahamas
February 12, 1874

CHAPTER ONE

My Military and Political History— Beginnings (1810-1822)

I HAVE, since my earliest years,[1] been drawn to the glorious career of arms, feeling it to be my true vocation and calling. On the ninth of June, in the year 1810, with my parents' blessing, I enlisted as a first-class cadet in the permanent infantry regiment of Vera Cruz. Thus, from the age of fourteen, I belonged to the Royal Army of New Spain. I had already proved my gentlemanly qualifications—an indispensable asset in those times.

Under the orders of Colonel Joaquin Arredondo,[2] the first battalion of my regiment was sent to pacify the eastern internal provinces of Mexico, and it fell my lot to be a participant in this five-year-long campaign. I had risen through the ranks to become Lieutenant of Grenadiers of the Second Battalion, and on November 20, 1815, I joined my company at Vera Cruz.

On the sleeve of my left arm I wore a decoration of honor—having distinguished myself in action.[3] The Governor of the Plaza, noting this honorable mark of a good officer upon me, appointed me military commander of the area outside the city. This area was under constant attack by local insurrectionists. My handling of this duty and other dangerous commissions so satisfied my commanding officer, that I soon wore on my shoulder, two epaulets—at last fulfilling a golden dream of my ardent youth.

The lower classes on the outskirts of Vera Cruz were committing all types of abuses under the guise of insurrection. Therefore, the commandant general of the province placed under my orders five-hundred seasoned veterans, with orders to stop all insurrection immediately.

I was a very punctilious soldier, and so I worked ardently and with a high degree of loyalty to fulfill the confidence and trust my commanding officer had placed in me. But, obeying my natural inclination, I more often than not resorted to persuasion, rather than to arms. By these means, I managed to bring about the surrender of the insurgents—more than two thousand armed and mounted men—who agreed to live in peace and to be obedient to the government.

The commandant general realized the importance of this service, and I was rewarded with a promotion to Lieutenant Colonel, receiving for my services the coveted *Cross of the Royal and Distinguished American Order of Isabella the Catholic*.

Installed as the principal commander of the now peaceful district and having ample authority, I built towns, rebuilt the Villa de Medellion, and tried to reorganize the district to the best of my ability. I accomplished my purpose to such an end, that, at the end of three years, the people, who had come from the mountains in a state bordering on savagery, now lived peacefully and had acquired admirable manners and customs.

I knew that I had been favored by the vice-regal government and I was very grateful. But, even so, when the *Plan de Iguala* was made public, by proclamation of Colonel Agustin Iturbide, on February 24, 1821, I hurried to sponsor it, wishing to contribute my own little grain of sand to our great political rebirth.[4]

Field Marshal Jose Davila—then Commandant-General, Superior Political Chief, and Intendant of the province—considered that I had merely strayed, but felt that I was in grave and immediate danger. Being of a generous and kindly nature, he decided to save me. He sent me both an amnesty and many coaxing offers of safe conduct, by means of the sergeant-major, one Ignacio Iberri.

The old general truly loved me as a son, and such kindness touched the strings of my heart! Ah, the painful moment of decision—the moment when I decided to turn aside his offers, remains fixed forever in my memory! But through this awesome struggle, this moment of trial, my patriotism overcame all other emotions. I clung resolutely to my purpose!

Setting all the flattery and temptations aside, I could see only a situation fraught with nearly insur-

9

mountable difficulties. I was surrounded by twelve thousand excellent soldiers stationed throughout Alvarado, Cordoba, Orizaba, Huatusco, Jalapa, Perote, Puente del Rey, and Vera Cruz. I knew that I would be forced to fight and conquer them all.

My supplies and support for the initial campaign consisted solely of one hundred twenty-six infantrymen, eight hundred horses taken from those who had deferments, one four-pound cannon, one ammunition box, some rifle cartridges, and a thousand pesos which I donated to the commissary from my own pocket.

It was truly a victory-or-death situation. If I wavered even slightly—I would be lost! My actions, therefore, were fearless, almost to the point of rashness.

Leading my small band of troops, I made the march of fourteen leagues to Alvarado without difficulty. Juan Topete, captain of the frigate and commander of the leeward coast, was so overcome with surprise that he hid himself at home. His forces, lacking a leader, made no move against me. Such a critical moment admitted no delay. I addressed those hesitant men with such firmness and zeal that when I finished, instead of hesitation, I was met with an exultant outburst of "Viva la Independencia!"

Everything was under my control: troops, fort, magazine, provisions, munitions—everything! This unexpected conquest of the Port of Alvarado created quite a sensation in the government and acted as a stimulant to the revolution. Both friend and foe admired my success and its resulting benefits to our goal of liberty.

Having increased my army and its provisions, I next rushed to the rescue of Lieutenant Colonel Jose Joaquin de Herrera, who was surrounded by three thousand royalists in Cordoba. Entrenched with a mere handful of revolutionary enthusiasts, Herrera was prepared to die fighting. My entry into Cordoba was timely; the patriots were entrenched behind their last wall, engaged in a fight to the death.

With a sheer disregard for the danger involved, I summoned some two thousand men and six cannons and rushed to the offensive. Again I was fortunate! Colonel Hevia, the famous Spanish leader of the Royalists, was not on the battlefield. The day was ours! The Royalists retreated in confusion to Puebla, leaving behind a group of deserters who sought refuge behind my banner—the tricolor!

After this rescue by my troops, Lieutenant Colonel Herrera marched with his forces to the province of Puebla, acquired reinforcements, and began again to campaign successfully. I, myself, marched to the city of Jalapa to attack Colonel Juan Orbegoso. After a successful onslaught by my troops which lasted six hours, Colonel Orbegoso's two thousand six hundred well-equipped troops surrendered. A third of his forces deserted to my side. With these reinforcements, my battalions were increasing daily.

I had only to make the initial proposition of surrender to Colonel Flores, commanding officer of

Puente del Rey, and the two forts were ours. Near El Paraje de Santa Gertrudis, we defeated a contingent of Colonel Concho's on their way to Perote from Puebla in search of food and ammunition. We then proceeded to besiege the Perote fortress for twenty-six days, until it fell.

During the campaign, I had ordered Lieutenant Colonel Juan N. Fernandez and four hundred of our choice troops to the province of Tabasco. Welcoming these reinforcements with open arms, the Tabascan revolutionaries proved victorious.

On July 30, 1821, the Spanish warship, *El Asia*, bearing the newly-appointed Viceroy of New Spain, Lieutenant General Juan O'Donoju, anchored at the port of Vera Cruz. The new Viceroy was shocked to find the plaza under assault and almost in our power. After watching the situation closely for three days, he called me to an interview with him at the Alameda.

The Viceroy proposed a compromise based on the *Plan de Iguala*, which he hoped would bring about better relations with the insurgents. His proposal satisfied me, but I hesitated to make any serious settlement without first conferring with our commanding general. I impressed upon the Viceroy the necessity of obtaining the approval of Iturbide, leader of the army of the "Three Guarantees," if we wished to obtain any permanent results. The Viceroy agreed, and I immediately communicated with Iturbide, informing him that O'Donoju had approved of my demands. I implored the Viceroy to come at once to Vera Cruz to meet with O'Donoju.

My trusted aide, Captain Jose Marino, delivered the message personally to Iturbide at the *Hacienda del Colorado,* three leagues from Queretaro. Our leader was so pleased that he extolled my virtues even to the point of flattery. He decided to proceed at once to Cordoba to welcome and confer with the Viceroy.

General O'Donoju agreed, and I personally assured him of his safety and of his treatment as a gentleman. He replied, pointing to the walls, "I am determined to go. And I am unafraid when escorted by the valiant soldier who assaulted these walls."

The Viceroy and Iturbide arrived at Cordoba on the same day. Upon their invitation, I attended and participated actively in their conference and its successful outcome. On the 24th day of August, 1821, they signed the famous *Treaty of Cordoba,* ending the war. High hopes were felt by all!

My own campaigning ended with the occupation of Vera Cruz. The garrison there, having no other alternative, retreated to the castle of Ulua. On October 6, to the sounds of rejoicing, I triumphantly entered Vera Cruz at the forefront of my victorious army.[5] I personally raised the tricolor over the town and was saluted with thundering blasts of artillery.[6] Such were the fruitful results of my seven months' campaign!

I here present this sketch of my part in helping to obtain my country's freedom, even though it is quite well known. I do so because some of my countrymen have tried to suppress and misrepresent my part.

THE EAGLE

Incredibly enough, those who are most determined to malign me are the very sons of the patriots who, literally overcome with joy, embraced me and blessed my name. Ah, what a change!

CHAPTER TWO

The Empire (1822-1823)— The Republic (1824-1825)

KING FERDINAND VII of Spain was so incensed by the *Plan de Iguala* and the *Treaty of Cordoba* that he ordered the official court executioner to burn them. General O'Donoju fell out of grace with his sovereign. At the same time, Iturbide succumbed to the flattery of those around him. The temptation was too great! He declared himself the occupant of the Throne of Montezuma.

Although Iturbide could not foresee it, his action was highly unpopular with the people and would soon lead to his loss of power and anarchy for the country. The people strongly favored a regency with lawmaking by means of representatives. I, myself, favored such a system, and I let my opinions in support of it be known.

About this time, the Republican Party came into being for the first time. It began to attract more and more people. Many of my friends tried to coax me into joining with them, but having been reared under a monarchy, I could not favor such an extreme change and listened to their words with disapproval.[1]

THE EAGLE

One night the Spaniards who controlled the castle of Ulua attacked Vera Cruz and attempted to destroy the bulwarks of Santiago and Concepcion.[2] Their surprise attack was a failure due to the vigilance of the guards, and the Spaniards sustained heavy losses in a two-hour battle. A Spanish general, three of their officers, and one hundred forty-six soldiers of the Cataluna battalion were captured. Our imperial government considered this a glorious victory and awarded me my commission as Brigadier General.[3]

On October 30, 1822, Emperor Augustin I (as Iturbide had declared himself) dissolved the elected Congress which had convened on February 24, declaring the Congress to be antagonistic to his imperial person. Soon thereafter he started for Jalapa, trying to draw me from my province, where I had come under denunciation of his friends.[4]

Knowing my disapproval of his coronation as Emperor,[5] "His Majesty" stripped me of my command and ordered my transfer to Mexico City, without extending to me the mere vestiges of courtesy.[6] Such a crushing blow offended my dignity as a soldier and further awakened me to the true nature of absolutism. I immediately resolved to fight against it at every turn and to restore to my nation its freedom.

I knew that my resolve would mean great effort and personal sacrifice, but I was determined to gain freedom at any price. I hastily made a public appearance in Vera Cruz in order to address the people. Before my troops, I proclaimed the Republic of

16

Mexico on the second of December, 1822. I published the *Plan de Vera Cruz* and a manifesto in which I expressed my intentions, carefully stating that these were only to be temporary, in order for the nation, itself, to be the true arbiter of its destiny.

My troops soon clashed with the imperial army under the command of General Jose A. Echavarri.[7] Several battles were fought—some favorable to my cause, and some unfavorable. Soon the superior numbers of his forces forced my troops back into the city, where we were constantly besieged.[8]

On the night of January 30, 1823, the Emperor ordered an assault to be made against my forces. In three hours time, we—although but fourteen hundred in number—fought our way to complete victory. The twelve thousand besiegers were so unskillfully generaled that our withering volleys routed them into a shameful retreat, leaving the surrounding battlefield strewn with the dead bodies of their soldiers.

To hide its shame, three days later the defeated army issued the ignominious *Plan de Casa Mata*, dated February 1, 1823.[9] This extraordinary event was destined to change the entire political complexion of the country, for two weeks later, on the nineteenth of February, discouraged by defeats and desertions, the Emperor abdicated his throne.

My victory could not possibly have been more splendid! Judge and jury that I was in these momentous times of the destiny of my country, I remained faithful to every promise in the program that I had proclaimed for the Republic. With a zeal that was almost religious in nature, I followed it to the letter![10]

On the eleventh of May, the ex-Emperor, Don Augustin Iturbide, and his family embarked from Vera Cruz for Italy. I ordered that all due respect should be paid to his departure.

By order of the Provisional Executive, in 1824, our nation selected its representatives in a completely free election for the first time. When the newly-elected Congress convened, it drew up the Constitution of 1824, which was approved and published by the provisional government after due deliberation.[11] The former provinces, now Sovereign States, free and independent, with all the privileges afforded them under the law, accepted the Constitution and elected as their President the patriot Guadalupe Victoria.[12]

However, all was not peaceful. In March of 1824, a revolution arose in Yucatan over local problems. Merida and Campeche were at war. The provisional government, then still in power, delegated me as Commander-in-Chief and ordered me to pacify the squabbles between the two cities.[13] With my staff I boarded the warship *La Iguala*, and we sailed in safety to the port at Campeche.

Cannons hailed my arrival into the port, and the jubilant people demonstrated in my honor. The military commandant, Lieutenant N. Roca, quickly placed himself at my command. The opposing colonel, Benito Aznar, who had been steadily besieging the city, quickly followed his example. Both the people of

Campeche and Merida overwhelmed me with honors, and the Provisional Junta elected me political governor of the entire province. By settling the differences between the cities in peace, I successfully established order and restored security to the region. I organized active committees and permanent governing bodies. In addition, I built up the fortifications, and, in every manner, I provided for the security of the province.[14]

About this time the sad news of the murder of Augustin Iturbide at Padilla reached me.[15] When the news spread through Merida, one of those peculiar tricks of human nature occurred. The lobby of the government house was filled with a cringing, power-hungry crowd. Full of smiles, they congratulated me on the death of the hated tyrant. Sickened at their cynical sentiments, I told them: "Gentlemen, if this nation can possibly derive any benefit from the tragic murder of the leader of Iguala, then offer your congratulations to the nation. But spare me your congratulations. Although I disagreed with his coronation and with him on the field of battle, I was never a personal enemy of Iturbide's. Had he come to Yucatan, I would have spared his life." The crowd retired in awe and confusion, but I could not stop the gossip that spread through the city for several days.

The heat of Yucatan sickened me, and I sought and received a transfer to the province of Vera Cruz. There, for more than two years, I lived in peace and tranquility, devoting all my attention to improving my personal estates at Manga de Clavo.[16]

19

CHAPTER THREE

The Election of Vicente Guerrero (1828)—The Spanish Invasion (1829)

IN THE YEAR 1828, a stormy election ensued. Manual G. Pedraza, Secretary of War, challenged the patriot of the people, General Vicente Guerrero, for the office of second constitutional President. Through skillful maneuvering and through the power his office gave him, Pedraza obtained one more vote in the legislature than Guerrero.[1] Depression and desperation followed Pedraza's election. Revolution was the natural result.

At the time of the election, I was in charge of the government of Vera Cruz. Nothing that I could do to preserve order in this grave situation was sufficient. I knew that revolution was inevitable!

In order to spare the lives of the people and to quell the whirlwind of revolution, I adhered to the pleadings of the people that Vicente Guerrero be declared constitutional President of the republic.

Pedraza's partisans declared me "outside the law," but it took me only three months to put down their attacks.[2] The popular movement became so strong that Pedraza fled in disguise to the United States. When order was finally restored, Guerrero, the people's candidate, was declared constitutional President.[3]

On the twenty-ninth of July, 1829, intending to reconquer Mexico, a division of the Spanish army, under the command of Brigadier General Isidro Barradas, landed at Cavo Rojo and proceeded to occupy Tampico and Fortin de la Barra without meeting any resistance. A valiant, but vain, attempt was made by true patriots to halt the Spanish invaders at Paso de los Conchos. Quickly the alarm spread throughout the nation.

The invaders passed through the territory under my control, and I was seized with patriotic fervor. I knew that the honor of leading the defense of my country lay in my hands. Hastily I made the necessary preparations and began my campaign.

After some difficulty, I sailed from the port of Vera Cruz with a brigantine, four schooners, some small craft, two thousand three hundred foot soldiers, and as much munitions as possible. I also sent six hundred well-mounted lancers up the coast. With the true patriot's fighting spirit, I set out to brave every hazard to seek out the invaders.[4]

I landed safely in La Barra de Tuxpan, sailing through the Spanish squadron cruising near Tampico under Admiral Laborde. In piraguas and canoes we crossed the Tameahua lagoon and proceeded forthwith to Tampico al Alto. Then we marched to Pueblo Viejo.

THE EAGLE

The invading general had successfully occupied the town of Villerias. Confident that he would receive reinforcements from Havana, he had left behind only a small garrison at his headquarters. This was a direct invitation for action on my part—an invitation I could hardly fail to accept.[5]

With a thousand soldiers under my command, I crossed the river under cover of darkness. However, the garrison stood vigilently, and our surprise attack was frustrated. I was forced to attack the entrenchments, finally requiring them to surrender. In the midst of the formal capitulation, the commander-in-chief with his entire army appeared at the city gates. Needless to say, it was an embarrassing moment for me, and I felt everyone's gaze on my face. For a few seconds, I did not know what to do.

Fortunately, luck was with me! An old general named Solomon was in command of the plaza, and despite his age, acted with unusual haste. He besieged me with foolish questions, and while he was doing so, the capitulation was drawn up. I fooled the old man by exaggerating the number of my forces, indicating that I had some twenty thousand men waiting for me at my headquarters in Pueblo Viejo. The commander-in-chief commanded old Solomon to tell him what was happening at my headquarters. The foolish old man gave him such an exaggerated picture of the situation, that the general, instead of attacking my small force, requested a parlay.

I was greatly surprised when I heard his terms.

22

He merely desired that I abandoñ his headquarters and that I set a date for further negotiations. I agreed immediately, as my situation was decidedly critical. Within the hour my troops had crossed the river to safety.

I refused to meet with the invading general, as I considered his proclamations of little value. Nevertheless, I thought it my duty to point out to him the rashness of his undertaking and to advise him to retreat at once. His reply was so ridiculous that it indicated to me the full measure of his incapacity. I declined to communicate with him any further.

Hostilities resumed immediately. My first act was to cut off the enemy's lines of communication and to see that they received no further assistance. Therefore, I planned to oust them at Fortin de la Barra, which was defended by ten pieces of artillery and four companies of the Crown Battalion. I captured the pass at Dona Cecilia, which lay across the river and between the enemy headquarters, and La Barra— within a single night, my troops were securely entrenched.

Leading fifteen hundred soldiers, I commanded the general to surrender. His haughty reply infuriated me, and I attacked his forces furiously, disregarding his entrenchments and barricades. A bloody battle, lasting eleven full hours, from six in the evening to five in the morning, ensued. When their boastful leader was wounded, he surrendered unconditionally.

The commander of the enemy army had remained

in his quarters throughout the entire battle. The constant pounding of our artillery and the fear of the twenty thousand men we had supposedly sent against his troops frightened him so that he sent Brigadier General Solomon to inform me of his surrender. At such surprising good fortune, I commented: "When fortune smiles on Santa Anna, she smiles fully!"

As the sun's rays spread over the banks of the Panuco River, the first Crown Division of the vanguard surrendered their arms and colors according to the rules of war—surrendering a force three times the size of my own. I permitted the officers to retain their swords. Thus, the destiny of Mexico was irrevocably assured on that memorable day!

When General Isidro Barradas was informed of the size of my forces at Pueblo Viejo, he cursed his error violently. His anguish aroused my pity. The poor man fell victim to his grief and died shortly thereafter in New Orleans.

As is the custom in Mexico, cheers and ovations greeted the conquering hero at every turn. The General Congress bestowed on me the title, *Benemerito de la patria*. I was promoted to General of Division and acquired the emblems of rank, which were pinned on me by General Manuel de Mier y Teran.[6] This impressive ceremony took place on the very place where the invaders had surrendered. I was voted swords of honor by the various legislatures, and the general public hailed me as, "Conqueror of Tampico."[7]

I felt that the country was entering a period of

peace, and I retired to my estates at Manga de Clavo for much needed rest, pleading to heaven that I would not have to answer another call to arms. But, unfortunately, I was mistaken—the uprisings continued unremittingly. General Anastasio Bustamente, Vice President of the Republic, led an uprising against President Vicente Guerrero, publishing the *Plan de Jalapa* and leading the troops of the reserve army. I stepped in immediately, demanding that Bustamente desist. But Bustamente aspired for power, and my protestations fell on deaf ears.[8]

Knowing that his troops were inferior in number to those of Bustamente, President Guerrero retreated to the mountains at the south, hoping to hold his position with arms. The Vice President, in his own words, "without shaking off the dust of the road," placed himself in command of the Presidency. He pleaded with me to come to his aid, but I refused.

Meanwhile, Bustamente's troops were actively pursuing those of Guerrero. A bloody battle ensued between the two armies, ending in an unforgettable and detestable event. The infamous Genoan, Picaluga, acting on the instructions of the Vice President, visited President Guerrero in Acapulco and invited him at his convenience to dine aboard his ship, then anchored in the harbor. He badgered the unfortunate Guerrero into accepting his offer, and while the President was enjoying his dinner, he was attacked by Picaluga's sailors, bound, and tossed into the wine cellar. Picaluga ordered the boat to lift anchor, and he sailed away with his prisoner. When he reached the port in Oaxaca, Picaluga dropped his prisoner and received fifty thousand pesos from the public treasury. Thus, the unscrupulous enemies of the patriot Guerrero sacrificed him without mercy![9]

CHAPTER FOUR

The Vera Cruz Act—
Pedraza Becomes President (1832)

THROUGHOUT the entire nation there rose a cry of indignation against the cruel and shameful treachery of the enemies of General Guerrero. Patriotic Vera Cruz was the first to issue a proclamation demanding the removal of the minister responsible for the act.

A commission from the city council called on me at my Manga de Clavo home, asking for my support. Their petition seemed just and fair, and I recommended it to the Vice President himself. Also I advised two of the ministers, Lucas Alaman and Antonio Facio, to conform to the growing public opinion. Hard-hearted and self-satisfied in their positions as these men were, they failed to see the wisdom of my pleas.[1] Their replies were arrogant and threatening, and without delay they ordered a strong division to Vera Cruz under the command of General Jose M. Calderon. Calderon was ordered "to restore order in the rebellious city." The people of Vera Cruz met this order with a zealous resolve to defend themselves, and they called on me to aid them in their cause.[2]

I could not remain indifferent to the demands of my fellow citizens nor to my own security, which was threatened by this invasion, and I took command of the defense of the city. The unhealthy climate of the region took its toll on Calderon's troops. As his sick list continued to grow, he was forced to cease hostilities and to retreat to Jalapa. Our forces swelled in number, as Calderon's abandoned sick joined us.

The ministers held firm to their position despite growing public opinion, and it became necessary to organize an army in the city of Orizaba. It was now too late to turn back the tide—the issue would be decided with guns!

Minister of War Facio positioned himself with an army of five thousand along the heights of Aculcingo, threatening Orizaba and hindering the entrance of my troops. I was forced to take the offensive, and I marched my poorly-provisioned forces along the dangerous slopes of Maltrata in order to surround the minister's troops from the rear. Frightened by my advance, Facio retreated toward the capital, strewing the roads with anything that would hinder a swift retreat. Being unable to overtake this "aggressive" Minister of War, I occupied Puebla, an important city, despite opposition from its daring Commandant General, Juan Andrade.

Meanwhile, the Vice President, campaigning in the interior, defeated General Stephen Moctezuma at the port of Gallinero. I waited for him at the Hacienda of Casa Blanca, and encountered him on his return from the capital. While our cannons were booming, a heavy hailstorm arose. Taking advantage of the inclement weather, the Vice President abandoned camp.

I followed him to the Rancho de Posadas, where he offered to fight again. Although he had gathered reinforcements from General Quintinar's division, he was completely defeated and fled to San Juan Hill. As I was gathering my forces, Manual G. Pedraza appeared at my camp and pressed me to abandon my pursuit. Pedraza was returning to the country as President, having been recognized by the state legislatures, and I was required to give in to his wishes.[3]

Pedraza's intervention paralyzed my operations, resulting in the *Plan de Zavaleta*. In compliance with the *Plan*, Vice President Bustamente and his ministers were turned over to the Supreme Court of Justice for trial, and Manual G. Pedraza assumed control of the government.[4]

Caricature of Santa Anna

Exmo. S. TEN. GRAL. D. JUAN O-DONOJÚ Sevill
Ultimo Virrey de Nueva España: prestó el Juramento en Veraci
n 3. de Agosto de 1821. Firmó los tratados de Cordova en
y murió en 8 de Oct. del mismo año

Juan O'Donoju, last Mexican Viceroy. Courtesy Dallas Historical Society.

Augustin I (Iturbide), Emperor of Mexico

Jose Joaquin de Herrera

General Santa Anna, from a print first published in the United States in 1837

General Manuel Mier y Teran

Jose Maria Tornel

Santa Anna's Hacienda in Jalapa

Vicente Guerrero

DISCURSO

PRONUNCIADO POR EL E. S. GENERAL DE DIVISION CIUDADANO

Antonio Lopez de Santa-Anna,

PRESIDENTE

DE LOS ESTADOS-UNIDOS MEXICANOS,

AL ABRIRSE SOLEMNEMENTE LAS SESIONES

DEL SESTO CONGRESO CONSTITUCIONAL.

━━━●❚◉❘◉❚◈❚❘◉❘◉❚◉●━━━

Ciudadanos diputados y senadores del congreso de la union.

La providencia nos concede, por un favor señalado, que comenceis á desempeñar vuestras augustas funciones, cuando la paz estiende sus beneficios por toda la republica, cuando los partidos y las facciones que la mantubieron en prólongada agonia, han perdido el funesto poder de convertir en principios los estravios de la razon, en acciones heroicas los crímenes mas espantosos. Encadenado ya el monstruo de la anarquia, los talentos y las virtudes republicanas cesaron de ser titulos de proscripcion; y aquel estado de instabilidad que no presentaba garantias sólidas de ninguna especie, ni á la sociedad, ni á sus individuos, se disipa finalmente, dejando en todos los corazones sensibles á los impulsos del amor á la patria, una avercion profunda á las ecsageraciones, á las estravagancias de una epoca de desorden y escarmiento.

Los directores de los negocios se entregaron imprudentemente á ilusiones de perfectibilidad, y desconociendo el prestigio de hábitos antiguos, la prevencion de los espiritus, la debilidad y complicacion de nuestra máquina social, le imprimieron un movimiento irregular que debió conducirla á su ultima ruina. La política, esa ciencia sublime, cuyo objeto es dirigir los intereses particulares al bien general, sirvió solamente para contrariar los intereses de todos, para erigir á la opresion en sistema de gobierno. Se olvidó que las verdades politicas y morales pasan lentamente por medio de los errores, que se desenvuelven poco á poco y que su fruto sazona por la tarda operacion del tiempo. Suponiendose que la ilustracion habia penetrado hasta en las masas del pueblo, se intentaron reformas que no habian sido discutidas ni analizadas de antemano, se plantearon con una violencia escandalosa, se apoyaron en la fuerza fisica, recurso único y efimero de las medidas que se separan de la opinion ó que la combaten. El gobierno se puso en guerra con sus propios súbditos, y estos sufrieron todas las vejaciones de una tirania desconcertada, á la vez que se invocaban los derechos santos de la justicia, los goces de una libertad racional y todos los bienes que mejoran y consolidan una sociedad civilizada.

Sorprendido el pueblo, arrastrado hácia una senda que veia lo llevaba al abismo, reflecciono sobre su suerte, palpó toda la estencion de sus peligros, apeló al enérgico recurso de su voluntad y de su poder. Se espera en vano sumision y obediencia de los pueblos, cuando se les considera como viles esclavos cuando el capricho de unos cuantos hombres célebres únicamente por su audacia, es la regla de las operaciones administrativas.

No es estraño, señores, que la indiferencia ó pasibilidad con que se dá en cara á nuestro pueblo, hubiera cambiadose derrepente en actitud hostil, y que una revolucion provocada de tantas maneras, estuviera á punto de inundar en sangre á nuestra infeliz pátria. Los tormentos de la sociedad se habian multiplicado, las persecuciones se succedian unas á otras, la propiedad era un motivo de ecsecracion, los talentos causa de ruina, y aun los grandes servicios á la nacion, titulo de oprobio y escalón quizá para un suplicio injusto, preparado secretamente por la mas negra ingratitud.

El rumor de la tempestad llegó al retiro que habia escogido para alejarme de la intervencion fastidiosa de los negocios públicos, para dar lecciones prácticas á los que tanta injusticia hicieron á mis sentimientos, de que el ejercicio del poder no es objeto digno de una alma verdaderamente republicana. En medio del universal conflicto se me señalaba como única esperanza de salud; los que observaron el desenfreno de los ódios y resentimientos, los que veian encendida la antorcha de la doble guerra civil y religiosa, me conjuraron con la instancia del grave peligro que amenazaba á la república, á que volase á su ayuda y á su socorro. No pude, no debi ser indiferente á la presencia de tantos males. Volvi á empuñar las riendas del gobierno en el momento crítico y preciso en que la sociedad se aprocsimaba á su disolucion.

En este tiempo se manifestó en la ciudad de Orizava, una chispa eléctrica que debia naturalmente generalizar el incendio para el que la imprudencia y la maldad habian acumulado tantos combustibles. Por una fa-

Proclamation issued by Santa Anna in 1835.

39

Martin Perfecto de Cos, Santa Anna's brother-in-law

General Sam Houston, from a drawing made about the time of the Texas Revolution

41

NEW YANKEE DOODLE.

St. Ana did a notion take, that he must rule the land, sir:
The Church and he forthwith agree to publish the command sir:
    In Mexico none shall be free—
    The people are too blind to see;
    They cannot share the liberty
    Of Yankee Doodle Dandy.

Ye Mexicans henceforth beware, my central plan attend to,
My shoulders will the burden-bear, no Yankee shall offend you.
    In Mexico none shall be free—
    The people are too blind to see;
    They cannot share the liberty
    Of Yankee Doodle Dandy.

Of soldiers now he stands in need, but soldiers must be paid, sir;
He then dictates a law with speed, to seize the Yankee trade, sir.
    In Mexico none shall be free—
    The people are too blind to see;
    They cannot share the liberty
    Of Yankee Doodle Dandy.

Obedient to their tyrant's will, his myrmidons comply, sir:
The Texians see along their coast, some vessels captured nigh, sir.
    In Mexico none shall be free—
    The people are too blind to see;
    They cannot share the liberty
    Of Yankee Doodle Dandy.

To Vera Cruz they send each prize, each unresisting man, sir;
Remonstrance, too, is found unwise, it makes the foe less bland, sir.
    In Mexico none shall be free—
    The people are too blind to see;
    They cannot share the liberty
    Of Yankee Doodle Dandy.

The pirate Thompson's next essay, brave Hurd to capture too, sir,
Resulted quite another way: such robbing will not do, sir.
    In Mexico none shall be free—
    The people are too blind to see;
    They cannot share the liberty
    Of Yankee Doodle Dandy.

The Texcans say they won't receive the central plan at all, sir,
And nobly go to meet the foe, with powder and with ball, sir.
    In Mexico none shall be free—
    The people are too blind to see;
    They cannot share the liberty
    Of Yankee Doodle Dandy.

Hurza! for Texas volunteers, we are the boys so handy,
We'll teach the Mexicans to fear our Yankee Doodle Dandy.
    Yankee Doodle let us hear,
    Yankee Doodle Dandy;
    We'll teach the Mexicans to fear
    Our Yankee Doodle Dandy.

By order of the Chairman of the Committee of Vigilance and Safety of this place, (Nacogdoches, Texas.) GOD AND LIBERTY.
    G. A. NIXON, *Chairman.*

D. E. LAWHON Printer, Nacogdoches.

Song played by Texan army at the Battle of San Jacinto. Unique broadside from the C. Dorman David collection.

42

The storming of the Alamo

General Sam Houston listening to the sound of the cannons at the Alamo, near Washington-on-the-Brazos. This picture appeared in an early biography of Houston. Washington-on-the-Brazos and the Alamo were many miles apart, and it would have been impossible for Houston to have heard any battle sounds.

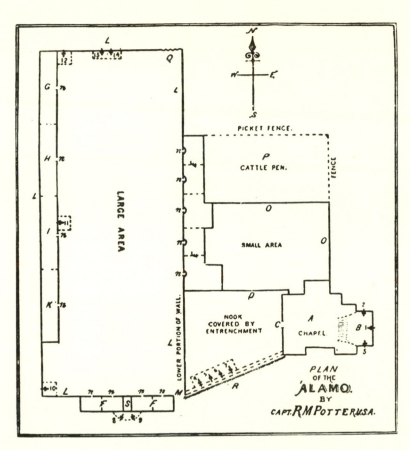

Ground Plan of the Alamo

CHAPTER FIVE

My Election as President—
The Texas Campaign (1833-1836)

BY THE FREE and unanimous election of the legislature, I was chosen constitutional President of the Republic. According to the provisions of the Constitution, I assumed my office in April of 1833,[1] despite the fact that I had not reached the age required by law.

I felt an intense desire to be worthy of the high confidence placed in me by the people as I took over my presidential duties. When there suddenly appeared an army under the command of Gabriel Duran, proclaiming "Religion and Rights," I knew that I must suppress this revolt at the very outset. I marched against Duran at the head of a division of soldiers and left Vice President Valentin Gomez Farias in charge of the country.

In Tenancingo, General Mariano Arista was made my second in command, an honor to which he responded with treason. Communicating secretly with the rebel leader Duran, Arista gave him invaluable information which assisted Duran in overpowering

me when we clashed near Cuautla (now Morelos).
I was imprisoned in a nearby hacienda, while Arista
gained control of my troops by proclaiming me a
dictator. Not recognizing Arista's perfidy, my troops
marched innocently under his command to Guanajuato.

General Duran informed me that if I would accept the dictatorship, he would be the first to obey
my command. In disgust, I replied: "The President
of the Republic, duly elected by the legislature, cannot be made a rebel!" My answer so angered him
that I was thrown into prison at his command and
surrounded with a heavy guard.[2]

During my absence, Vice President Gomez Farias
acted with both loyalty and discretion. He sent
Colonel Geronimo Cardona in disguise to my prison
to aid me in escaping. Such a skillful and determined
man needed no further instructions. With the assistance of the manager of the estate, he succeeded
in getting me past my guards. I escaped at nine
o'clock in the evening, and without losing a moment,
I mounted the horse which had been provided for
me and struck out for Puebla. Colonel Cardona and
I arrived safely, and there I was offered a carriage
and escort to carry me to the capital.

In order to stop Arista's scandalous acts and to
prevent their spreading further, I marched six thousand men to Guanajuato, where the rebel was still
in revolt. Cholera morbus had just penetrated into
Mexico, and a terrible epidemic struck my troops

47

while we were passing through the heavy rains in the Bajio. The dread disease ravaged and incapacitated a third of my force, causing me to countermarch to Allende, where the epidemic had not struck. I remained in Allende during the worse part of the season, replenished my troops, and continued on to Guanajuato, which was also free of cholera.

Protected by strong fortifications and assisted by the division leaders whom he had coaxed to his side, Arista believed he could defeat my government troops and save himself. But his efforts were in vain. Within three days, I had defeated him and taken him prisoner. His compatriot Duran escaped to Guatemala, where he died.

When I returned to the capital, I encountered stormy sessions of the Congress. One faction was endeavoring to confiscate the property of the church and to deny to the clergy its rights and ancient privileges. The public was dismayed by these actions and opposed violently any usurpation of the clergy's rights. Obeying the dictates of my conscience and hoping to quell a revolution, I declined to approve the necessary decree to put these edicts into law.[3]

The members of Congress who held an interest in the decree were easily swayed and agreed to stay in the background. However, they soon realized that the people had no confidence in their self-renunciation and they continued their arguments, converting the Congress into a battlefield. The members demanded that the Governor of the Palace turn over to them the keys to the salons, which they had left open. However, he refused them, saying sardonically, "Gentlemen, since you have deserted the cause, you are dismissed."

These careless reforms of the Congress caused turmoil among the people. In Cuernavaca a *Plan* was issued and swiftly accepted by all the states. Under this *Plan*, the President was granted extraordinary powers.[4] Meanwhile, Congress was able to convene, and once more the government gained the people's confidence and was able to preserve the peace.

In 1835, the colonists of Texas, citizens of the United States, declared themselves in open revolution and proclaimed independence from Mexico. These colonists were in possession of the vast and rich lands which an earlier Mexican Congress—with an unbelievable lack of discretion—had given them.[5] In declaring themselves independent, they claimed that other favors, which they demanded, had not been granted them.[6]

They had no difficulty in receiving aid from New Orleans, Mobile, and other parts of the United States.[7] These filibusters combined in such great numbers that the commanding general of Texas, Martin P. de Cos,[8] found himself imperiled in San Antonio de Bexar and was forced to capitulate, leaving the colonists and filibusters in possession of the entire state.

I, as chief executive of the government, zealous in the fulfillment of my duties to my country, declared that I would maintain the territorial integrity whatever the cost. This would make it necessary to initiate a tedious campaign under a capable leader immediately. With the fires of patriotism in my heart and dominated by a noble ambition to save my country, I took pride in being the first to strike in defense of the independence, honor, and rights of my nation. Stimulated by these courageous feelings, I took command of the campain myself, preferring the uncertainties of war to the easy and much-coveted life of the palace.

Congress named General Miguel Barragan to the office of President *ad interim*, while I personally assembled and organized an expeditionary army of eight thousand men in Saltillo. A serious illness confined me to quarters for two weeks, but after my recovery, I resolved not to lose a day. The ox-carts carrying our equipment slowed us down considerably, and we were forced to ford rivers on rafts. Lack of provisions hindered us in our journey across the desert, and plants and wild animals provided the rations for our army. Nevertheless, there were no complaints on the part of the soldiers, and this army well deserves the gratitude of the nation.

Our army's crossing into Texas was the cause of great surprise on the part of the filibusters, for they believed that Mexican soldiers would not cross again into Texas. Frightened by our invasion, they ran to a fortress called the Alamo,[9] a solid fortress erected by the Spaniards. A garrison of six hundred men under the command of Travis, a leader of some renown

50

among the filibusters, mounted eighteen cannons of various calibers. Confident that aid would come, Travis replied to my proposition of surrender, "I would rather die than surrender to the Mexicans!"[10]

The self-styled "General," Samuel Houston,[11] said to the celebrated Travis, in a letter we intercepted: "Take courage and hold out at all risks, as I am coming to your assistance with two thousand men and eight well-manned cannons." We did not hesitate to take advantage of this information that fell into our hands.[12]

I felt that delay would only hinder us,[13] and ordered an immediate attack. The filibusters, as was their plan, defended themselves relentlessly. Not one soldier showed signs of desiring to surrender, and with fierceness and valor, they died fighting.[14] Their determined defense lasted for four hours, and I found it necessary to call in my reserve forces to defeat them. We suffered more than a thousand dead or wounded,[15] but when the battle was over, not a single man in the Alamo was left alive. At the battle's end, the fort was a terrible sight to behold; it would have moved less sensitive men than myself. Houston, upon hearing of the defeat of the men at the Alamo, rapidly retreated.

General Jose Urrea's brigade utterly defeated Colonel Fancy [Fannin][16] near Goliad. Fancy had occupied Goliad and met Urrea with fifteen hundred adventurers and six cannons. Urrea hailed his triumph over Fancy in a dispatch, which ended: "As these

51

filibusters entered Texas with arms to assist the colonists in their revolt, they were judged outlaws and all prisoners have been shot."[17] This action was based on a law passed November 27, 1835, in compliance with which the war in Texas was waged "without quarter."[18]

Our stay in Bexar did not last long. General Ramirez Sesma pursued the retreating Houston, sending the following dispatch from the Colorado River: "There is nothing new happening in my brigade. The filibuster Houston and his gang remain waiting on the other side of the river. His movements indicate that he plans hostilities, and I feel that reinforcements are a necessary precaution." I immediately sent a strong division to Sesma's aid and followed behind them myself. Houston, learning of the approaching Mexican army, completely disappeared. With his men deserting him in droves,[19] Houston was planning no attacks against our forces.

I planned to advance swiftly against the rebellious colonists, as I felt that the campaign should be finished before the spring floods. The heavily guarded Brazos River lay between me and my enemy. We surprised a small enemy force at Thompson's Crossing and crossed the river safely on captured rafts.

Some five leagues farther on lay the village of Arrisburg [Harrisburg], the seat of government of the self-styled "Republic of Texas." Not a minute could be lost! I marched directly toward the town with six companies of men and a small cannon.

Under cover of night, we crossed the prairie and were approaching the town's edge when a gun accidentally discharged. The explosion aroused the dogs and the local citizenry, who ran to hide in a little steamer which they had left with engine running. They made their escape up Buffalo Bayou, a stream flowing into the San Jacinto River around Galveston Island.[20]

A letter from Houston was found in the residence of I. Bonnen, [David G. Burnet] the titular President of the so-called "Republic of Texas." Houston's letter related that he was indeed in low spirits: "The catastrophies of the Alamo and Goliad, and the grievous loss of Travis and Fancy, have discouraged our men and they are deserting in large numbers, fearing that the cause of Texas is lost. I intend to use the first vessel that enters the San Jacinto River to seek haven on Galveston Island for the time being. The Mexican army continues to advance, and our government must be ever mindful of its duty."[21]

I considered it expedient to pursue Houston and, at the same time, equally important to increase my personal forces. I ordered my second-in-command, General Vicente Filisola, who waited with a large force at Thompson's Crossing for Urrea's brigade, to bring his forces and another battalion to meet me immediately. I had left Filisola two special orders in writing: First, he was not to send me any written communications which might be intercepted by the enemy. Second, after joining with Urrea, he was to hurry his army to overtake me. My orders, dictated

53

with a good deal of forethought and timeliness, did not prevent a deplorable event which Filisola's disobedience brought about. His tardiness deliberately caused the disgrace of a highly successful campaign.[22]

Realizing that Filisola had failed to overtake my army, I resolved not to lose a single hour. I searched for Houston's forces along the San Jacinto River and located him under a forest shelter, about to retreat to Galveston. I decided to delay his retreat until Filisola's forces or the battalion of engineers arrived. I camped within view of the Texans and was waiting impatiently when General Cos and three hundred recruits from the Guerrera battalion under Manuel Cespedes arrived.[23]

Disgusted at having my orders disobeyed and foreseeing disaster, I decided to countermarch at once and to seek the reinforcements Filisola was to bring me. Alas! It was already too late. The evil had been done. The disobedient Filisola had sent one of his aides in search of me to deliver communications from Mexico. Houston captured the messenger and tortured him before he could reach my camp.[24] The knave told all that he knew. When Houston found that his forces were superior to mine, he took courage and planned his attack.

At two o'clock of a hot afternoon, April 21, 1836, I lay sleeping in the shade of an oak tree, hoping for cooler weather to begin my countermarch.[25] The filibusters surprised my camp with admirable skill,[26] and I opened my eyes to find myself surrounded by their rifles and my person in danger.[27] The responsibility for my capture rested solely with Filisola. He, and he alone, had caused the catastrophe by his criminal disobedience. He failed to advance even when Urrea's brigade joined him. His failure to act seemed to be in anticipation of some event which was never to come. When he learned of the disaster at San Jacinto, he became all action at last.

Unfortunately, he failed to come to the assistance of the prisoners, but rather abandoned them to their fate. He fled pell mell toward Matamoras, one hundred seventy leagues away, abandoning honor, duty, and humanity. Even the filibusters criticized his conduct. Fearing a severe reprisal, he published a profuse declaration, so inaccurate and false that no one paid it any serious attention.[28] His true conduct in Texas was well known.

Samuel Houston treated us in a way that could hardly have been hoped for. His humane and generous conduct contrasted severely with that of Filisola. Recognizing me, he addressed me courteously and offered his hand. Despite the wounds he had received in the assault on my camp, he showed deep concern for me and ordered my cot and tent placed near his own.

Houston allowed my aide, Colonel Almonte,[29] who spoke fluent English, to serve as interpreter between us. He said to those of his men who demanded revenge against us: "There is no need to resent these prisoners. They acted under the law of their government." I have always remembered with gratitude and appreciation how much I owed to this remarkable man in the darkest moments of my career.

Houston left a few days later for New Orleans to receive treatment for his wounds, leaving in command the so-called "General" Rox [Rusk],[30] whose conduct was completely the opposite of Houston's. This villian confined me, under guard, at the ranch of Orozimba.[31] Furthermore, he threw me and my interpreter, Colonel Almonte, into chains. My treatment at the hands of Rox encouraged the colonists to clamor for my execution, in order to prevent another revolution. They fought to get at me and discharged pistols at my prison door.

My disastrous situation changed with the return of Houston. On seeing me imprisoned, he charged Rox with barbarian cruelty and ordered my chains removed. He sent me much-needed food, and with touching words, he begged me to forgive Rox's insolent behavior. He assured me that Rox had already been reprimanded.

When he left me, Houston said with deep emotion: "General, you are no longer a prisoner. From this moment, you are at absolute liberty. I ask only one favor in exchange for my kindness to you. Before returning to your country, I implore you to visit President Andrew Jackson, my protector and friend. He will receive you with kindness, as he wishes to make your acquaintance."[32]

In despair at my helpless state and fearing that I

would never escape from the filibusters, I could hardly refuse him. With good grace, I offered gladly to comply with his wishes.

On November 16 of the same year, 1836, I began the journey to Washington, accompanied by two of Houston's aides and my own aide, Colonel Almonte. We crossed the Sabine River, the boundary of Texas, and traveled through unsettled territory until we reached the Mississippi River. We traveled in the *Tennessee* up the Mississippi for twenty days, then continued up the Ohio River, landing close to Louisville. There we gathered provisions and proceeded to Washington through heavy snow storms.

General Andrew Jackson greeted me warmly and honored me at a dinner attended by notables of all countries. He placed at my disposal for my voyage to Vera Cruz a battleship, whose commander attended me with great respect.

President Jackson was keenly interested in the outcome of the war with Mexico. He told me, "If Mexico will recognize the independence of Texas, we will indemnify your country with six million pesos."

I replied to him: "To the Mexican Congress solely belongs the right to decide that question."[33]

CHAPTER SIX

My Resignation as President—
The Defense of Vera Cruz (1837-1838)

O NCE MORE in the bosom of my family in the pleasant seclusion of Manga de Clavo, I thanked God for delivering me from the hands of my enemies when I was betrayed by Filisola. I resolved to abandon political life and officially resigned as President of Mexico.

I was disillusioned and resentful. It seemed that my country had abandoned me to my enemies. In my intense grief, I vowed, "No longer is it just for my family to share my sacrifices."

I was grateful for the solitude and peacefulness of Manga de Clavo. I busied myself with domestic life, which seemed, in my melancholy state, as welcome as a desert oasis to the weary traveler! Ah, but soon my peace was shattered! And how much it was to cost me! But how does one escape one's destiny? And what a fatal destiny and what bitter days to come!

The events which follow are difficult for me to describe, for even now they have a profound effect on me. How can they not fail to affect even the most indifferent reader!

I was enjoying the contented life of family man, with no distractions, when unexpectedly my tranquility was destroyed. A French squadron appeared near Vera Cruz and discharged its cannons over the fortress of Ulua. King Louis Philippe of France felt he could abuse Mexico, as she did not have a military force equal to his.[1]

Honor declared that I accept the challenge. Justice was on the side of Mexico! We must meet force with force! Now that the conflict had begun, it was the duty of every loyal Mexican to protect his flag. I knew that I was wearing the sword of Mexico and the insignia of a general, and I was not engaged in the national struggle. As if by magic, I seemed to forget all the wrongs my country had done me. It could not be otherwise, as love for my country had been uppermost in my heart from an early age. Carried away with the same enthusiasm which had first driven me into battle, I hurried to the combat field. I presented myself to Commandant Manuel Rincon, and my services were quickly accepted.

Rincon ordered me to inspect the fortress of Ulua, and I crossed over to it in a small boat under protection of darkness. I inspected the batteries, magazines, war material, and provisions. I particularly noted the spirit of the commander and his troops. In my opinion, everything was in a deplorable state![2]

General Gaona, commander of the fortress, wanted

to surrender to the French, claiming that Rincon had been negligent in sending him reinforcements. Everyone revealed his disheartened condition and greatly exaggerated the incompetence of the soldiers. I was thoroughly disgusted with what I had seen and closed my ears against further reports. To every man I pointed out his duties in these dangerous moments and retired from the fortress.

I informed Rincon of the events at Ulua and advised him to send other officials and additional provisions to the fortress under cover of darkness. However, he, too, was in favor of surrendering to the French. Unable to prevent such a shame, I returned to Manga de Clavo.

And it happened just that way. Vera Cruz and Ulua surrendered, and the French flag waved over their walls. The people rose up in arms over such a disgrace. They bombarded the President's palace, clamoring for Santa Anna, the "Conqueror of Tampico," to defend Vera Cruz.[3]

The President granted them their petition and named me commanding general instead of Rincon. He sent word to General Arista to place himself at my service with the brigade he was bringing to defend the fortress of Vera Cruz. President Bustamente had lifted the banishment from Arista and returned him to the army.

The President's orders reached me at ten o'clock on the evening of December 3, and, in response to the honor and confidence placed in me, I arrived in Vera

Cruz at seven the next morning. My aide, a corporal, and four lancers followed me. Rincon marched immediately to the capital, and I, despite numerous difficulties, devoted myself to the task at hand.

The Prince of Joinville with some members of the French squadron were residing in the city. He sent two French officers to inquire why I had returned to the city. To their inquiries, I was quite proud to answer: "The government of Mexico disapproves heartily of the surrender of this fortress, and General Rincon has been recalled to stand trial. From now on, I am commanding general here under orders of the government. I shall inform the admiral of your fleet of my orders in due time. In the meantime, I request that the Prince of Joinville and all other soldiers of France retire to the French squadron. If any French soldiers remain on land after one hour has passed, they shall be my prisoners."

I indicated my watch which showed eight o'clock. "You must be out of the fortress by nine," I informed them. The two officials looked at each other, saluted me, and left. The Prince with his soldiers left the fortress immediately.

The second and ninth battalions remained in their quarters, along with the active squadrons. The units of the national guard, however, returned to their villages disgusted at the surrender of the fortress.

At eleven o'clock that morning I received a dispatch from General Arista, stating that he had arrived at Santa Fe in compliance with my orders. I replied

61

to him instantly, ordering him to advance at nightfall to Los Pocitos which was in cannon range of the fortress. There he was to wait for new orders from me.

At seven o'clock that evening, Arista with his aide presented himself to me. I received him cordially, thinking he had merely anticipated my command. However, I became impatient with him when I found that his brigade was still at Santa Fe and that he had come merely to receive his orders from me.

I ordered him to proceed to Los Pocitos with his brigade at once. What an artful deceiver this man was! He pretended to be overcome with remorse for having offended me, and, in a pleading manner, he begged me to allow him to rest as he had been twenty-six continuous hours in the saddle.

I consented to allow him to rest for two hours. At nine o'clock he came to see me again, pretending this time that he was just ready to leave. Since he found me alone, he seized the opportunity to try to explain his actions at Tenancingo and Guanajuato.

The clock struck eleven, and, angered at his procrastination, I stood up and ordered him: "March at once!" With his right hand covering his breast, Arista replied seriously: "My General, be calm. I am sure that my lieutenant will carry out all orders. However, I am leaving right now."

With such honest words, how could I doubt him? However, Arista deceived me. He had my orders in his pocket at that time, and he did not even make a pretense at beginning the march. I was exceedingly anxious and slept little that night. At four-thirty in the morning, the shouts and gunfire of the advance sentinels swung me into action.

With sword in hand, I leaped down the stairs searching for my guard. The guard was located in an adjoining building, already engaged in battle with the French.

I immediately saw that we were outnumbered and ordered a retreat to the barracks. Admiral Baudin, his lieutenant, and the Prince of Joinville had penetrated the plaza in three places. The Prince, with four hundred marines under his command, proceeded to my quarters in hopes of capturing me. While searching for me, they encountered Arista, Colonel Jimenz, my aide, and my valet. Disappointed at not finding me, the Prince said, "Well, he's missed a chance of going to Paris to be educated."[4]

Forcing the barracks to surrender seemed an easy task to the Admiral, but after five hours of fighting, he realized his mistake. I knew that chance favored me, and I was not one to overlook a chance of doing a good service for my country.[5]

I knew that the enemy believed us to be weak, and, leading a column of five hundred soldiers, I started out to overtake them. I was hoping to keep them from their ships and oblige them to surrender. Not knowing that the scoundrel Arista had spent the night under my very roof, laughing at my orders, I was counting on help from his brigade.

63

The French were fleeing for their boats. An eight-pound cannon protected their rear guard. When we attempted to take it, they discharged it, wounding me seriously. Their cannon fire also wounded Colonel Campones, my aide, another officer, and seven grenadiers. As we charged, the French abandoned the cannon, little realizing the serious damage they had done.

I remained unconscious for two hours. When I recovered, I realized my situation and was terrified. I was stretched out in the flag room of the principal barrack. The bones in the calf of my left leg were mangled, one finger of my right hand was broken, and my entire body was covered with bruises. No one thought that I would live to see another dawn.

I, too, thought I was dead! Ah, how we deceive ourselves! I rejoiced in the enthusiasm that we had a decided advantage over our enemy, who had thought our forces could not measure up to his. I prayed to God to let me die in a blaze of glory. How many times since have I bewailed that fact that God failed to accept my humble pleas!

But the ways of The Almighty are wondrous! My unworthy life was spared, while the nine men wounded with me died shortly afterward. Also, the five surgeons who had operated on me and held no hope for my recovery went to their deaths.[6]

CHAPTER SEVEN

The Revolution—The Presidency Again—Exile (1841-1844)

SIXTY-TWO DAYS after my foot had been amputated, General Guadalupe Victoria called on me at the instigation of the government. He informed me that a revolution was threatening, and that the government desired me to take Bustamente's place as temporary president in these times of trials.[1] How well the people knew me! They knew I would never desert my principles and would always be on hand when my country needed me!

I was carried to the capital on a litter. Although my trip was made with extreme care, the hardships of the journey and the change of climate weakened me. However, despite my poor health, I assumed the office of President immediately. The tasks involved completely overwhelmed me, but without ill results. The government forces triumphed throughout the country. General Gabriel Valencia captured and executed the hope of the revolution, Jose A. Mejia, in the vicinity of the town of Acajeta. The dreaded threat of revolution died, and peace was restored.

THE EAGLE

Bustamente once again took up the reins of government, and I retired to Manga de Clavo to complete my recovery. However, Bustamente's loss of prestige with the people caused his government to fail. In the town of Guadalajara, in the early months of 1841, arrangements were made for Bustamente to abdicate and for the reform of the Constitution of 1824. In Tacubaya, a council of generals agreed upon a set of provisional bases to help bring about these reforms, and once again I assumed the office of provisional President.[2]

During the period in which the country was governed under the *Bases Provisionales de Tacubaya*,[3] peace was preserved without a single tear being shed for political reasons. There was no graft, no forced loans, nor any government misappropriations. The government employees, widows, and pensioners received their incomes on time, as did the bond holders. During this period the first railroad built in Mexico —running from Vera Cruz to the interior—was contracted for and begun.

Many other reforms and municipal projects were begun during this time. The market of the capital was built, the great *Santa Anna Theatre*, the customs house, and the greater part of the pier at Vera Cruz. The old Parian was demolished, and the copper coin, so harmful to commerce because it could be counterfeited so easily, went out of existence. In addition, our foreign relations were carefully cultivated, and the country extended its territory by annexing Soconusco. All of these works are well known throughout the country.[4]

In order to conform to public opinion, I called together a junta of prominent citizens from all states in the nation to instigate needed reforms. This group drew up *Las Bases de Organizacion Politica* on June 12, 1844. This constitution was circulated by the government, and each of the states accepted and ratified it without dissension.

In September of 1844, my beloved wife died. Greater sorrow I had never known! General of Division Valentin Canalizo substituted for me while I devoted myself to family matters.[5]

During the first session under our new Constitution, I was duly elected President and called to the capital to administer the customary oath. The election saddened me. My deep melancholy drove me to abhor the glamorous life of the capital and to prefer a life of solitude. I resigned the noble office to which I had been called, but the public intruded upon my privacy, pleading that I return. My friends, with the greatest of good faith, also begged me to resume my office. Their pleas led me to sacrifice myself to the public good. I withdrew my resignation.

Near the last of October, General Paredes rebelled against the government in Guadalajara. When the news was communicated to me by the government, they ordered me to take the troops quartered in Jalapa and march to the capital. I instantly followed the full instructions of the orders.

67

Paredes had been relieved of his command of the Capital District due to excesses of intoxication while he was commanding his troops. He bore a grudge and was determined to take revenge. In our country one spark was sufficient to set aflame a revolution.[6]

I was marching toward Guadalajara under orders, when I received the news of an upheaval in the capital and of the imprisonment of Canalizo, the President *ad interim*.[7] The situation seemed serious, and I stopped my march at Villa de Silao.

The details of the revolt in the capital arrived soon after my halt. The infamous words the messenger read me are repeated here:

"The majority of Congress openly favor the Paredes revolution. The government, in self-defense or wishing to avoid revolution, has issued a decree by which the sessions of Congress were suspended and the Constitutional President invested with extraordinary powers. This decree has served as a pretext for General Jose T. de Herrera to rise against the current government, a service for which he was rewarded with the appointment of *interim* President. The rioters imprisoned President Canalizo and extended their aversion to the President, Santa Anna. They tore down a bronze bust erected in his honor in the *Plaza del Mercado*. They stripped his name from the *Santa Anna Theatre*, substituting for it *The*

National Theatre. Furthermore, they have taken his amputated foot from the cemetary of Santa Paula and proceeded to drag it through the streets to the sounds of savage laughter and regaling . . . ."

I interrupted the narrator, exclaiming savagely, "Stop! I don't wish to hear any more! Almighty God! A member of my body, lost in the service of my country, dragged from the funeral urn, broken into bits to be made sport of in such a barbaric manner!" In that moment of grief and frenzy, I decided to leave my native country, object of my dreams and of my disillusions, for all time.

At the head of eleven thousand well-trained and well-armed men and with partisans in the capital, I could have taken it easily. However, I was drained of all vengence and was determined merely to leave my country forever. I countermarched toward Puebla, avoiding everyone.

The Commandant General of Puebla, Ignacio Inclan, had supported the revolution in the capital, failing in his previous oath of loyalty to the government. Therefore, it was necessary for the army to camp outside the city until further arrangements could be made.

I sent General Ignacio Sierra y Rosso to the capital to submit my resignation to Congress and to arrange for my passport to leave the country. It seemed logical to me that the revolutionary President would be happy to see me leave the country. Therefore, I was determined to leave the army, and I set out for the port. This mistake was to cost me dearly.

It was not possible for me to leave without first saying farewell to the comrades who had been loyal to me through many campaigns. They gathered in formation, and I addressed them from my horse.

"Companions in arms," I stated, "with pride I lost my leg in the service of my country. Many of you were with me on that sad occasion. Now, however, that pride has turned to grief, sadness, and desperation. I want you to know that this leg I sacrificed for my country has been torn from its funeral casket and dragged through the public streets to be made mockery of. I see that you are both shocked and shamed. You are right! This type of violence is foreign to your natures. I am leaving you, following my destiny. On foreign shores, I shall remember you always. I trust that each of you will always be loyal to your country. May God be with you."

This speech, delivered without any preparation, reveals my agitation and confusion at the time. In order to avoid compromises, I made another grave error. In Las Vigas, believing that my person would be respected, I discharged the convoy of hussars which accompanied me. I was traveling with only two of my servants, when I was halted in the town of Xico[8] by the commander of the Nationalists. He had been ordered by the Commandant General of the District of Jalapa to intercept me and send me under heavy guard to him. He kept me *incommunicado* and surrounded by guards, a virtual prisoner, in the municipal building for four days. Finally I was transferred to the castle of Perote.

The Commandant of the District of Jalapa was my former trusted friend, General Jose Rincon. He had flattered me and gained my confidence. I had trusted him so far as to leave my hacienda, *El Encero*, in his hands during my absence. On seeing how the revolution was going and considering me lost, he became frightened and joined the revolutionists, who were cursing me. Ah! What a miserable creature! And, what a coincidence! He would be dying when the people of Jalapa would be celebrating my return to the country with joyful demonstrations.

The so-called "conquerors" held me captive for four months in Perote, but, as they found me disturbing, they condemned me to exile. I was notified that if I returned to Mexico on my own accord, I would be declared "outside the law."[9]

San Antonio de Bexar (1835–1836)

The Alamo, 1837

Vicente Filisola

David G. Burnet

Thomas J. Rusk, Secretary of War, during the Texas Revolution

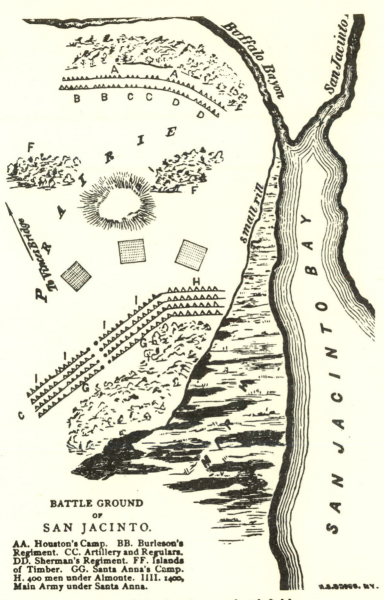

BATTLE GROUND
OF
SAN JACINTO.

AA. Houston's Camp. BB. Burleson's
Regiment. CC. Artillery and Regulars.
DD. Sherman's Regiment. FF. Islands
of Timber. GG. Santa Anna's Camp.
H. 400 men under Almonte. IIII. 1400,
Main Army under Santa Anna.

Map of the San Jacinto battlefield

Mexican flag, captured at San Jacinto. Courtesy Dallas Historical Society.

H. A. McArdle's painting of the Battle of San Jacinto. Note girl sitting in front of Santa Anna's tent, bottom right.

American political cartoon, depicting Santa Anna surrendering his sword to Sam Houston

General Sam Houston receives the captured Santa Anna in the Texan camp at San Jacinto.

W. H. Huddle's painting of the surrender of Santa Anna

Sam Houston at San Jacinto

THE EAGLE

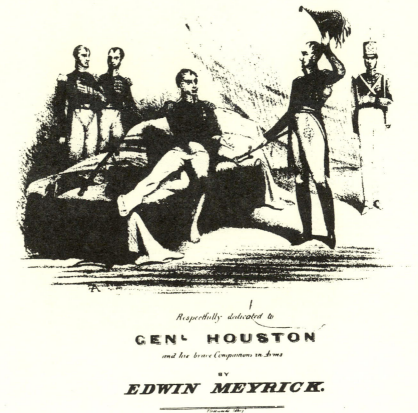

Cover of sheet music written shortly after the Battle of San Jacinto. C. Dorman David collection.

84

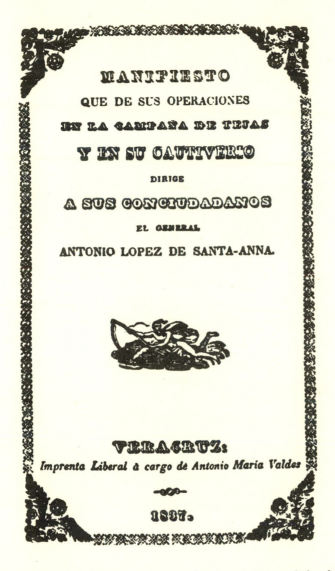

Title page from *Manifesto* issued by Santa Anna, defending his operations during the Texas Revolution

85

DIARIO

DE LAS

OPERACIONES MILITARES

DE LA DIVISION

QUE AL MANDO DEL GENERAL

JOSE URREA

HIZO LA CAMPANA DE TEJAS.

PUBLICALO SU AUTOR

CON ALGUNAS OBSERVACIONES PARA VINDICARSE AN-
TE SUS CONCIUDADANOS.

———

VICTORIA DE DURANGO 1838.

IMPRENTA DEL GOBIERNO A CARGO DE MANUEL GONZALEZ.

Facsimile of the Spanish title page

Title page from General Jose Urrea's diary of the Texas
campaign

86

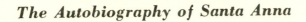

BIOGRAFÍA

DEL

GENERAL SANTA-ANNA.

MÉXICO: 1849.

IMPRENTA DE VICENTE GARCIA TORRES.

An early biography of Santa Anna

87

CHAPTER EIGHT

The United States Invades Mexico— My Return and Final Campaign (1845-1848)

ON MAY 19, 1845,[1] I left Mexico on an English packet boat, and, after fifteen days, arrived at the port of Havana. On learning that I was on board the packet, the Captain General of Havana, Leopoldo O'Donnell, was kind enough to invite me ashore. He sent his aide with his own boat to bring me to Havana. Although I had planned to continue on to Caracas, Venezuela, I could not ignore such hospitality. My family and I landed in Havana. General O'Donnell did honor to the position which he held, and his conduct to me was so gracious that I decided to reside in Havana.

While I was there, the government of the United States, having annexed the province of Texas, coveted the rich and vast territories of Alta California and New Mexico.[2] The United States government was well prepared to acquire the territories and swooped down on her sister and neighbor, Mexico, already torn by civil wars. The scandal and injustice of such a move did not matter. The United States had the forces, and that was all that was needed. General Zacarias [Zachary] Taylor moved against the Mexican troops along the frontier, defeating them at Palo Alto and Resaca de la Palma,³ owing to the bungling of the incompetent General Arista. When war was declared, faithful Mexicans recalled me to head the army.⁴

No veteran of the War for Independence could refuse a call to arms for his beloved country. No matter how humble my services might be, I answered the call. I chartered a ship—paying all expenses from my own purse—and sailed to Vera Cruz, defying the blockade.⁵ We sailed into the port on September 12,⁶ 1846, causing a sensation. What a change from my last look at Vera Cruz. The applause of the people let me know they had forgotten that fatal December 6.⁷ I journeyed to the capital amidst a continuous ovation, and my heart was overjoyed.

However, the affairs of the state were sad indeed! The Treasury was completely depleted, and the amount coming in could not even cover the necessary expenses. There was not even an army to meet the enemy. Our best men had been defeated on the frontier, and another regiment, under orders from General Pedro Ampudia, had surrendered in Monterey. The sad remainder of the army was scattered over the countryside. The mere handful of troops in the capital could not move for lack of equipment. And through all of this deplorable state of affairs, General Taylor triumphantly advanced toward the capital. But my faith held firm, and I renounced all hope of personal gain for the task at hand.

I felt that San Luis Potosi was a strategic point in the campaign, and I immediately marched there and set up my headquarters. Quickly we began to prepare for the battle. Only one thing bothered me. I was constantly puzzled as to how to meet the necessary expenses.

Previously, the General Treasury of the nation had supplied the commissary of the army with the basic necessities for each soldier. Now there was no money to supply these needed essentials, and each day our needs increased. The government answered my entreaties with false hopes and evasions. The soldiers grew more anxious with each passing day. "No one wants to send even bread and meat to the army," they grumbled.

To put the crowning touch to the situation and to try my patience to the end, a traitorous faction began circulating ugly rumors. "General Santa Anna is conspiring with the enemy! The enemy allowed him to enter the country! Santa Anna is a traitor to Mexico!" With its usual good sense and feeling for justice, the army ignored such ridiculous rumors.

Harassed on every side, I racked my brain searching for a way out. Victory was the only answer. I knew that if we did not move, we were dead. Victory was the only way out.

The enemy forces showed no signs of advancing. They had lost their best cavalrymen in a recent surprise attack at the *Hacienda de la Encarnacion.*[8] I knew I would have to surprise and fight them in sections. I had made up my mind to march in search of the enemy.

However, there was no money, and my action was impossible. I knew that I would have to make personal sacrifices for my country's safety, and I did not hesitate. I had the Mint coin a hundred bars of silver, giving as collateral the sum total of the property I owned—worth half a million pesos. The General Treasury paid the one hundred thousand pesos value of the silver plus the interest. The state commisary asked for an additional forty-six thousand pesos to cover a month's budget, and I ordered my agent, Dionisio J. de Velasco, to pay this sum to them. By my efforts, in January of 1847, the inhabitants of San Luis Potosi could survey a well-equipped, thoroughly instructed army of some eighteen thousand men, marching in four divisions in search of the invaders. The citizens of the town no longer need fear, for we left the city well garrisoned.

The leaders of the army did their best to train the rough men who volunteered, but they could do little to inspire them with patriotism for the glorious country they were honored to serve. And it was painful to see the number of deserters—some four thousand men in all. It was even more painful to find that one of these miserable men frustrated all my plans, rendering useless so many sacrifices, almost at the moment when victory was in sight.

When I reviewed the troops under my command at the *Hacienda de la Encarnacion,* I was pleased with their good condition, despite the number of deserters. As the troops marched back to camp, one soldier, Francisco Valdes, taking advantage of the approaching nightfall, deserted the army, taking two horses from the company. As he was heading toward his hometown of Saltillo, he was captured and taken before General Taylor. The traitor Valdes offered General Taylor important information concerning our troops, if he would be allowed to continue his journey in safety. General Taylor granted him his request, and Valdes revealed all he knew of our troops and plans.

Taylor had underestimated the Mexican army and was surprised to learn that they were so near. Using his information to advantage, Taylor concentrated his forces at the advantageous position of La Angostura.

From this vantage point, Taylor swiftly defeated three camps, composed of over nine thousand men. These troops had been stationed in a triangle at Saltillo, Vaqueria, and Agua Nueva. Without the information he had obtained from the informer, Taylor could not have won such an easy victory.

How the hand of fate frustrated my aspirations and hopes! Surely the invaders were saying to themselves, "Heaven watches over us!"

I cannot express the despair which gripped me when I witnessed the deserted camp at Agua Nueva.[9]

I could not imagine what had taken place, nor that a deserter from my own camp had warned the enemy. I bitterly regretted the many sacrifices we had already made, and I was further puzzled when the leader of our scouting party handed me a piece of paper with these words: "General, the enemy troops are ready for battle at La Angostura."[10]

Honor and duty commanded that we encounter them. During the days of February 22 and 23, a bloody battle ensued. Our recruits followed their brave leaders into the very heat of battle. Taylor was driven back, losing three cannons, a field forge, three flags, and more than two thousand dead, wounded, and prisoners. He managed to escape a decisive defeat on the second day of battle. My troops lost more than fifteen hundred dead and wounded, counting three generals. My horse was shot from beneath me, but I escaped injury and mounted another to resume my duties.[11]

The battle was going our way, and everyone in our camp felt that victory would be ours the following day. We were confident of our success. But, how things change! Suddenly our confidence turned to grief and despair. By word of mouth, the news traveled to our camp—revolution in the capital!

A special messenger was dispatched from the government to send the news to us. The government ordered our troops back to defend the capital and to restore law and order. The Minister of War was adamant; the army must return.

93

THE EAGLE

I was weary and bewildered by the unexpected orders. I ordered a junta of generals to decide the issue. When I had rested, I conferred with the junta and agreed with their decision. They felt that duty called for us to follow the orders of the government. I approved their decision, and our army began its long march to the capital the following day.

Our provisions were running short, and we needed to get rid of some four hundred prisoners who demanded both food and care.

I decided to demonstrate my generosity to General Taylor by sending him his prisoners. The General appreciated my concern and gave our Chief of Convoy a bed in his tent for the night. The General, himself, told our Chief of Convoy of the information he had received from the infamous deserter, confessing frankly that he owed his escape to this information. Our Chief of Convoy spoke English and had no trouble in understanding this terrible news.

Our march to the capital disgusted all the troops. Sadness and despair were reflected in their faces. The government repeated its orders, and the marches began. I proceeded at the head of the troops, followed by my Chief of Staff and a solitary squadron.

I traveled long distances every day, arriving shortly in the city of Guadalupe Hidalgo. When I arrived, the revolutionary activity halted. The terrorists recognized me as their President and obeyed my orders to lay down their arms and retire to their homes.

Exercising my rights as President of the Republic, I granted a generous amnesty in the name of the country. I called upon Mexicans of all political beliefs to rally around the nation's flag and unite against the common enemy in order to save the nation. With peace in the capital, things were back to normal.

I was preparing to return to San Luis when another fateful dispatch reached me. The governor of the state of Vera Cruz informed me of the following news: "I am sorry to report to the President that the fortress of Ulua and the plaza of Vera Cruz have fallen into the power of the American General, Winfield Scott. Our Commandant General, Juan Morales, has surrendered to him without giving battle, despite the fact that he had six thousand good soldiers capable of holding the plaza until reinforcements could arrive. General Scott stands at the head of a large army." So, one event followed another in plunging our country into turmoil.[12]

On studying the situation in the invaded region, I found that the invader had a clear march into the heart of the country. My heart trembled at the consequences! I knew I must preserve the honor of the nation by, at least, making an effort to block the enemy's route. It seemed to me that the course of greatest danger was preferable. General Pedro Araya was named President *ad interim* by the Congress in order that I might lead the expedition against the invaders.

I decided to encounter the enemy at Cerro Gordo.

95

It was located outside Vera Cruz on the highway that the enemy would take. I studied the position of the land, and stationed my troops there. As there were no fortifications in the area, peons from my estate, *Hacienda del Encero*, went to work to clear the grounds. The Lieutenant Colonel of Engineers, Manuel M. Robles Pezuela, began work on the fortifications at once. Reinforcements and troops arrived immediately, cannons were hoisted to the battlements, and trenches were dug. Our action continued until the enemy attacked us after only four days work.

General Scott moved fast, knowing that passage through Cerro Gordo would be difficult and costly if our troops and fortifications were in good shape. One of his divisions attempted to capture the Cerro del Telegrafo, but failed. The troops retreated, leaving the bodies of their dead strewn over the ground. Alarmed by the loss of his soldiers, Scott attacked with the full strength of his forces on the following morning.

Our four thousand untrained militia men defended the fortress valiantly for five hours. However, they were pitted against fourteen hundred trained veterans with heavy armament. Our troops put up a noble fight, causing considerable losses among the enemy, but were forced to retire in defeat.

When General Scott reported the capture of Cerro Gordo to his government, he greatly exaggerated the number of our troops and further added that he had driven us from our positions at bayonet point.[13]

I retreated to the city of Orizaba, where my troops were joined by twelve hundred men under the command of General Antonio Leon. With these men, I set out to defend our threatened capital. I encountered Scott's vanguard, under the command of General Wort [Worth], at Amozoc.[14] The vanguard attempted to detain us by heavily shelling our troops, but we managed to arrive in Puebla before them.

The leaders of Puebla had already decided to meet the enemy on friendly terms, and, mistaking my troops for those of Wort, sent a delegation in a luxurious carriage to meet us. Surprised upon recognizing me, the commission admitted their error. The mayor of the city had posted notices of surrender all over the city, and I found the entire situation intolerable. When I protested to Governor Rafael Inzunza and General Cosme Furlong, they stated that they considered surrender necessary in light of the fact that they had not counted on reinforcements to save the citizens from violence.

Disgusted with such cowardice, I began my march again. But the situation in the capital was no better. When we, the defenders of the country's honor and integrity, entered the city, the people cried, "You have only come to compromise us!" But the hour of trial was upon us, and all our strength was needed.

In order to learn the feelings of the leaders of the community, I called a meeting in the main room of the palace. I begged this delegation for courage, pouring out all the bitterness in my heart. Words

97

straight from the heart always carry more weight, and I moved the hearts of those men in such a manner that they enthusiastically agreed to sustain the honor and integrity of our dear nation.

After deciding how our capital should be defended, Congress closed its session, leaving all powers to the President. Our needs were great, and our efforts, of necessity, had to be great. It was an almost impossible task to ready the capital for a state of siege.

We began by organizing the troops into platoons —no small task, as over twenty-two thousand men were pouring into the capital. Over one hundred cannons of various calibers were built, arsenals were supplied, and uniforms and saddles were made. Fortifications were built all around the city, and strong palisades were constructed in the principal streets. After three months of hard work, the capital was in order to defend itself against the enemy.

However, all my efforts seemed to antagonize the traitors within the capital. One faction felt that peace at all costs was necessary and intrigued to have the people with money hide in order to evade making loans and donations to the army. The people, themselves, plunged into an indifferent state, totally ignoring the necessity for defense. All of this occurred while Scott occupied Puebla. While he remainded there, our preparations continued. In August when he appeared in the valley of Mexico with twenty-four thousand men, he found us ready for him.

98

General Scott examined El Penon, the primary entrance to the capital, and found it impractical for his purposes. He retired to Mexicalcingo[15] and later moved to the *Hacienda de San Antonio*. Neither of these entrances proved practical, and Scott's army halted a short way from the capital at the city of Tlalpam.

From the very beginning of the war with the United States, misfortune weighed upon the Mexican army. The happenings which follow will bear out this statement.

General Gabriel Valencia was quartered in the town of San Angel with a strong division of five thousand men and thirty cannons. Agents for the traitors in the capital persuaded him that his troops were strong enough to overthrow the present government and gain the office of the President for himself. Valencia, swayed by flattery and a desire for power, enlisted his troops in his own behalf. As if to force Scott to action, Valencia moved his army to Padierna,[16] a place he thought was impregnable. When I found out that Valencia had defected, I realized what the action involved and set about to evade the threat in every way possible.

With four thousand reserves, I set out in search of Valencia. I was detained at San Angel by ten hours of continuous rain. I could not sleep all night long, but arose to find a beautiful dawn announcing a sunny day. I set out immediately with reinforcements from the Rangel Brigade. But our efforts were in vain.

99

Scott realized his good fortune, and moved quickly to surround Valencia's troops. Striking at dawn, he defeated Valencia shamefully. My seasoned troops moved quickly to check with heroic efforts Scott's triumphal march to the capital.

Fighting still while in retreat, I arrived at heavily fortified Churubusco, where I confronted Scott's troops. The firing continued from nine in the morning until five in the afternoon. Leaving the strength of the enemy somewhat reduced, I fell back to the plaza for the night. The battle of Churubusco was a glorious one for the Mexicans.[17]

When the invading army failed to move the next morning, we realized the toll our forces had taken. General Scott appealed to me to hear a commission from Washington, which had arrived at his camp. I would not have even listened to such a request if it had not been necessary to repair the catastrophe of Padierna.[18] If it had not been for the traitor Valencia, the enemy would still have been in the valley of Mexico. When Scott wrote to his government about the fortifications of the capital, he said: "We owed to the protection of God, and to nothing else, having come out so well from the undertaking."

What are the greatest of human desires worth when they are pitted against the fortunes of destiny? For the fortunate invaders was reserved the gold of California; for the Mexicans, misfortune.

A "cease fire" was ordered by the Mexican commission composed of Jose Ramon Pacheco, General

Jose J. Herrera, Bernardo Couto, and General Ignacio Mora y Villamil. After several conferences and lengthy discussions, the two commissions agreed to nothing. The exaggerated demands of the Washington government were ridiculous. They were not satisfied with gaining the vast territory of Texas, but further demanded indemnity.[19] They demanded the extensive region of New Mexico, all of upper California, and half the Republic for a mere twenty-six million pesos.

Since no agreement could be reached, fighting resumed without restraint. Territory was gained inch by inch. Blood was shed by the gallons. Dead bodies littered the battlefields. The soldiers of Mexico advanced with valor and glory.

On the eighth of September, we dealt the enemy a severe blow at Molino del Rey.[20] In twenty minutes we cut down more than a thousand men and sent the enemy fleeing in disorder to Tacubaya.[21] If at this moment General Juan Alvarez had sounded the charge, our defeat of the enemy would have been complete. Alvarez had been given definite orders to charge when he had the enemy flanked and within rifle range. But, as if he had nothing in the world to do, Alvarez remained as a spectator mounted on his mule. The leaders of the cavalry, knowing their honor to be at stake by such a foolish performance, demanded that "such a scandalous deed be judged in the council of generals." But circumstances did not permit such a judgment. However, I realized my error in

101

having placed the cavalry under command of such an incapable general and immediately ordered him dismissed from the army.

Another crucial event helped the enemy the following day. If such an error had not occurred, the enemy would never have been able to save himself. Much as I dislike to reproach the dead, I must relate the truth of the events as they occurred.

Francisco Iturbe, a man of infinite wealth, having failed to contribute any of his money to the war effort, sent private information to General Jose Maria Tornel, my quartermaster. It never bothered Iturbe whether or not his information was accurate. Iturbe sent the following message to Tornel: "I am sure that the enemy is going to enter the city tonight by way of the San Lazaro sentry post. Activity is already underway. Let this be a warning."

I had not anticipated such a movement from the enemy, but I could not ignore such a warning. I ordered General Antonio Vizcayno [Vizcaino] to guard the crossroads in front of the sentry post of Candelaria. This was the route the enemy would have to take if they were to proceed to the sentry post of San Lazaro. I also ordered General Ignacio Martinez, commander of Candelaria, to be on the lookout for the enemy's approach and to come to the aid of General Vizcayno in any way that he could.

I had thought that the enemy would first assault Chapultepec in order to gain easy access to the capital. I had planned to engage the enemy in action at

Molino del Rey, while my vanguard was covered at Chapultepec. If it had not been for the fatal advice of Iturbe, all of my movable forces with seventy cannons would have been assembled at Molino del Rey on the morning of the eighth. If I had followed my plans, all would have gone well. Our strongest force would have met the enemy, but I followed Iturbe's warning—a warning seemingly planned to save the enemy—and only two brigades of infantry and a battery of eight pieces encountered them. The others were on their way to San Lazaro. And with the changing of the forces, it happened that I was sleeping that night at the palace, instead of at Chapultepec.

All of our attenion focused on the sentry posts of Candelaria and San Lazaro. General Vizcayno came to me at four o'clock in the morning. He was extremely upset and told me: "My General, the invading army is now in front of the Candelaria. I have seen them with my very eyes."

How could I have doubted so serious a message uttered by a general? I truly believed it and marched in the direction of the Candelaria sentry post.

You can imagine my surprise when General Martinez said to me, "There is no change in the file under my command."

"Why not?" I asked. "Isn't the enemy approaching from the front?"

"No, sir," he replied. "The scout has just returned and reported that the enemy is not in sight."

103

THE EAGLE

I presumed that General Vizcayno was among the men who had accompanied me. I called for him, and, receiving no answer, I ordered a search for him. He was not to be found. Vizcayno's mysterious and incomprehensible conduct at this time can best be called treason rather than error.

While we were searching for Vizcayno, we heard the sounds of cannons from the direction of Chapultepec. I knew then that the attack was exactly as I had previously planned for it. I immediately ordered all forces to move to the aid of that region, and I marched swiftly in the same direction.

Although we marched as quickly as possible, we arrived just as the battle was ending. The brave generals, Antonio Leon and Francisco Perez, from their vantage point at Molino del Rey were able to check the enemy's advance to Chapultepec and force them to retreat, abandoning their dead.

If General Alvarez had followed orders and proceeded with his division during the disorder in the enemy's ranks, the Mexican army's day would have been a glorious one. The entire fault lies in the lack of action by Alvarez.

Arriving at Molino del Rey, my sorrowful eyes fell on two stretchers bearing the brave General Leon and the intrepid Colonel Balderas, both gravely wounded. Their two courageous battalions had lost two officers and eighty-six soldiers.

As you can tell, only Providence saved the enemy from complete disaster at our hands. It is only logical to assume that if a mere four thousand soldiers with only eight cannons could check and repulse him, he might have been completely routed if we had sent more than twelve thousand infantrymen and fifty-two cannons against him.

The defeat of the eighth of September weighed so heavily on General Scott that he considered withdrawing to Puebla to recover his health (or so he said). He would have done just this if the Council of Generals he conferred with had not opposed this action. It is interesting to note what this same Council had to say about my military operations when they considered the suggestion of a retreat. I repeat these words—words which made them my praisers, although that was not their intention. I shall repeat only part of them, as modesty forbids my repeating them all. The last words of the famous General Smith[22] are sufficient to show the high regard in which they held me. He said, "If we turn our backs on that man, we will never arrive in Puebla. I am not in favor of the retreat."

I am not repeating the accolades of the enemy in order to be boastful or presumptuous. I merely state them that they may stand alongside the evil accusations of one Deputy Ramon Gamboa,[23] first presented on August 27, 1847, and again repeated before Congress in Quertaro on November 17. These accusations of treason were presented against the leader, who in the saddest days of our country, was defending his country's honor from one end of the Republic to another—sacrificing all personal glory for this one aim. So if I state the words of the enemy, it is only in my self-defense. Comparisons between the statements will show fairness and justice on the part of the enemy; falseness, deceit, and madness on the part of Gamboa.

Scott, spurred on by his companions, struck again. He bombarded Chapultepec and took it four days later at the cost of many lives to our forces. The invaders, encouraged by this victory, attacked the sentry posts at Betlehen [Belen] and San Cosme. We resisted the attack, but treason aided them in obtaining a victory.[24]

I was at the Betlehen sentry post, when an aide arrived from the forces at San Cosme. He implored me, "My General, if you do not come to the aid of the sentry post at San Cosme, we will lose it. The enemy forces are large, and my commander is in urgent need of reinforcements."

I immediately ordered General Andres Terres to hold the entrenched lines under his command and set out for San Cosme with the reserve division and five howitzers. I succeeded in forcing back the enemy to such a point that they could not be seen. They left the battlefield scattered with their dead.

Our forces had scarcely caught their breaths when another aide arrived from the capital informing me that the Betlehen sentry post had been abandoned to the enemy. Although I doubted the seriousness of the message, I returned as quickly as possible. I was greatly surprised to see the enemy forces penetrating the Paseo Nuevo and attempting to enter the Citadel. A bloody battle to defend the Citadel began, and our greatest effort was needed to force the enemy back to the Betlehen sentry post. The enemy entrenched itself at the sentry post. I attacked twice but failed to dislodge the invaders.

I was anxious to learn how the enemy had taken the Betlehen sentry post and sent for General Terres. Strangely enough, no one in the garrison had seen him. I reproached Lieutenant Colonel Castro, the head of the second active Battalion of Mexico, for abandoning the post. "General Terres," he replied, "commanded me to take up my position on the principal plaza. As nothing was happening there, I returned here on hearing the enemy's guns."

When I questioned Colonel Arguelles, commander of the advance guard, he replied, "General Terres ordered me to the Alameda. It was my duty to obey his orders."

When I questioned Colonel Perdigon Garay, commander of another active battalion, he answered, "At the command of General Terres, I took up a position at the hermitage of La Piedad. When I saw that the enemy was entering the city, I hurried here."

The artillerymen verified the fact that General Terres had ordered them to transfer to the Citadel. All of these accusations verified the treason of General Terres.[25]

General Terres soon presented himself before me.

107

He was clothed in the uniform of the Mexican army and bedecked with the medals a generous Mexican nation had awarded him. I was angered and indignant at his arrogance. The blood pounded in my temples at the mere sight of him, and I threw myself at him, tearing the epaulets from his shoulders and striking him across the face with my horsewhip.

It was a mad, violent act, completely foreign to my natural inclinations. But I was completely overcome with fury at that ungrateful wretch who had betrayed my miserable country. I was disgusted by my actions, but, at least, I had spared the villain's life. Treason of this kind is usually punished by hanging. And, after all, Terres had not been born in the Republic.

Although we encountered so many difficulties, we managed to continue our defense of the capital without interruption. At eight that night I finally dismounted my horse to preside over a junta of war with the generals at the Citadel. The situation was very grave.

Tired, hungry, and with my uniform tattered by the enemy's bullets, I discussed the grave situation with the junta of generals for three hours. During the entire session I was bowed down with pain. Each of the generals took the floor in turn. Each general bitterly deplored the lack of enthusiasm the people showed toward the war. The soldiers were the only ones fulfilling their duties, although they had not been paid for several days.

108

The generals felt that it was useless to continue to defend the city without the people's support. They also felt that the people would be spared useless sacrifices if we surrendered. For these reasons and other insignificant ones, the junta unanimously agreed to withdraw from the capital. They felt that the national honor had been upheld by our defense and that it was impossible to defend the capital after the surrender of the Betlehan sentry post. They also felt it the duty of the defenders of the capital not to involve the people in any unnecessary dangers. The junta ordered all forces with their artillery to march at daylight the following day to Guadalupe Hidalgo, leaving the capital under the command of the governor. It would be the governor's duty to protect the rights of the people and to obtain a guarantee of these rights from the enemy leader. Acting in accord with the junta's decisions, I issued the orders and they were carried out.

The invading army, considerably diminished in numbers, occupied the city. General Scott maintained troops in the principal plaza during the time I was in Guadalupe Hidalgo, arranging for the necessities of campaigning. Scott thought I intended some blow to him when I retreated from the city. In the midst of such disasters, my constant thoughts, however, were centered on the interests of my country.

I knew how important it was to be prepared for the next campaign. In a junta of ministers I agreed to place Manuel de la Pena y Pena, President of the

109

Supreme Court, in charge of the country's affairs during the war.[26] He was to maintain his residence in the city of Queretaro. Free from the cares of the government, I dedicated myself completely to the campaign at hand.

Under the new plan of operation, I marched to Puebla, where the enemy had quartered a garrison of twelve hundred men and a good deal of artillery.[27] My object was to first take this enemy garrison and to cut off all communication from the port of Vera Cruz to the capital. To make a long story short, I approached the entrenched garrison carefully with forces under the capable leadership of General Don Joaquin Rea.

Through enemy deserters we learned that the besieged people were discontented and desired to surrender. Everything was favorable for their capitulation, as Scott did not have the forces to aid them, and mine were increasing day by day. However, I received a dispatch from the governor of Vera Cruz, reading: "I hasten to inform you that five thousand United States troops, ready for marching, have landed. They do not deny that their object is to aid the garrison at Puebla. They have set out for Puebla this very day."

As these forces were marching hurriedly toward Puebla, I set out with three thousand cavalrymen and six light cannons, hoping to stop the troops before they reached their destination. I spent the night near the town of Humantla and learned from the people fleeing from the invading army of the excesses which the enemy troops were committing. This news caused me to spend a sleepless night, and I arose at five in the morning. Although I was early, the enemy had left an hour before I arrived in Humantla. My scouts discovered eleven enemy soldiers who had stayed behind to pillage the town. We swiftly put them to death with our swords. My men pursued the enemy, and, taking advantage of their disorderly march, killed or wounded a hundred forty-two of their men. Their commander, General Lanne [Lane],[28] feared my cavalry and ordered his troops to halt.

His infantry took refuge behind their carts, which they set up in a square. Silent and terrified, the enemy crouched behind the carts, listening to the yelps and cries of my cavalry.

Our sense of well-being was increased when General Isidro Reyes arrived with his brigade and two twenty-six-pound cannons. We knew victory was within our grasp, and no one doubted that we would defeat the enemy on the following day. However, our elation at four that afternoon had turned to sadness and despair by five. God's will must be done.

There are many events in these *Memoirs* which will provoke doubt on the part of the reader, because the reader may have never heard of them before. There will also be those events which will provoke the reader's wrath and indignation because of the treachery of those events. Surely, the events which follow will provoke the reader's strongest indignation.

111

THE EAGLE

Pena y Pena's Minister of Foreign Relations Luis de la Rosa was quartered in Queretaro. By special aide, he sent me the following orders: "His Excellency, President *ad interim*, is aware of the general clamor for peace. He wishes for hostilities to stop immediately on our part, and, until further disposition, the troops under your command, will remain under the orders of the General of Division, Manuel Rincon. Your Excellency may retire to a place of convenience for you to await further orders . . . ."

The mere reading of such a disgraceful order—an incredible order in view of the nearness of the enemy—swelled me with anger. My teeth were so tightly clenched that I could hardly utter a word. Observing my condition, General Reyes asked me with surprise, "My General, what is the matter?"

My first emotion subsiding somewhat, I found my tongue. I bitterly deplored the misfortunes of my sad country, betrayed at every turning, and disgraced by the very sons to whom she looked for loyalty and support. I handed General Reyes the dispatch from de la Rosa, sighing, "Read this and you will be convinced that God's wrath seems to weigh upon our wretched country . . . ."

Reyes quickly read the dispatch, and when he had finished, cried desperately, "My General, this is treason! Let's march to Queretaro and shoot the traitors!"

Thoroughly dejected, the division of cavalry left its imposing position and marched toward Humantla.

At nine that evening I called the captains to my quarters and informed them of the orders I had received—orders, which commanded us to retreat just when we seemed in a position to defeat the enemy. With sighs and entreaties, they begged: "This demands instant punishment, General. Let's hasten to Queretaro to prevent this disgraceful sale of our country's honor."

Completely disillusioned, I had to inform them of my final decision, made after much pondering on the situation. "Gentlemen," I said, "I was called to defend my country when our enemies invaded our territory. It has been my most fervent and honest desire that, in some feeble way, I might be useful to my country. Life, honor, family, property—all that man holds most dear—I have dedicated to the fulfillment of this desire. In the past I have raised armies and led them from one end of the country to the other to fight our country's enemies—no matter how large the enemy army might be.

"It is my fervent wish that I might have died fighting for my country. If I had, I would never have had to witness this sad spectacle. What treachery! Who would have believed that the man I trusted and raised to power would betray that trust! Who would believe that he could cease the fighting and relieve me of my command of the army! My friends, I have lost faith in our country and its leaders. My services in her behalf have ended. I shall leave the army and the country, so that I will not be a witness to the

113

shame to come. You will be prepared, I am sure, to witness the fact that the sword was wrenched from my grasp in the very face of the enemy's attack. So, I choose to comply with the orders of the Provisional Government. In view of the absence of General Manuel Rincon, who is still in the capital, I turn my troops over to the command of the worthy General Isidro Reyes. My friends, with my heart torn with sorrow and suffering, I bid you a final farewell."

The captains listened to my words in silence. Many were moved to tears. All tried to convince me to stay, but I had made up my mind. There was no going back.

I was filled with contempt for the conduct of Manuel Pena y Pena and was bitterly anguished at having trusted him. But how was I to know from his spotless past that he was involved with the traitorous faction which was dedicated to peace at any price? How could I judge a man who had always enjoyed a reputation of honesty and truthfulness? Some things one cannot believe without the evidence of them.

I carefully composed my reply to Minister de la Rosa. "The orders of His Excellency, the President *ad interim*, were unexpected, to say the least. To suspend hostilities with the enemy at this point is extremely dangerous to the country from every standpoint. As to my being relieved of my command of the army, I must protest that it is scandalous, despotic, and illegal in every sense. However, in the presence of an invading army, patriotism for one's country demands that one avoid any scandal or dissension from which the enemy could gain an advantage.[29]

"It is for this reason that I choose to obey the order. However, I obey the order under extreme protest. I shall leave to the President *ad interim* the immense responsibility which he incurs by his orders. I do not desire to witness my country's humiliation, and so I ask only for a passport, which I hope to receive when I arrive in Tehuacan."

General Rea lifted the siege at Puebla and with his troops retreated to Matamoras de Izucar. The auxiliary forces escaped defeat and entered Puebla. When I had attended to my affairs, I left for Tehuacan, escorted by a squadron of hussars.

The war that the United States unjustly began in our country would not have ended as it did, if treachery had not taken the place of patriotism. In my voluntary exile, I comforted myself by the thought that I had done all in my power to rid my country of her enemies. I would never have participated in the shameful and sorrowful *Treaty of Guadalupe Hidalgo.*

My Attempted Assassination—I Leave for Jamaica (1848)—My Return to Power (1850-1853)

MY ENEMIES, or rather the enemies of my country, stopped at nothing in trying to harm me. In every man there exists a feeling for justice, and I shall relate here three infamous deeds, which surely will horrify the reader. The first, which I have mentioned before, was Ramon Gamboa's accusation of treason against me in the chamber of deputies. The second is my attempted assassination by the invaders in Tehuacan. And the third is my being refused refuge in Oaxaca. It is easy to see from these deeds the conditions which surrounded me in those unfortunate days.

The first deed was the work of the Minister of Foreign Relations, Luis de la Rosa. He merely used his deputy, Gamboa, as a tool for his evil deeds. When Gamboa lay dying in the capital in 1855, he begged me to pardon him. He implored me to forgive him through his confessor, a San Franciscan priest, saying that the injury done me was weighing on his conscience. He insisted that he had accused me of treason only at the insistence of his political party.

The second infamous deed is not well known. It still remains a mystery and should be explained. I was waiting in Tehuacan for my passport to leave the country. One night the Prefect arrived at my house greatly excited. He handed me a paper that he had just received. The message read: "Senor Prefect. To-day, at dawn, five hundred well-equipped Yankee soldiers arrived at my estate. They tried to miss being seen, but I suspect they are headed for the city. I wish to inform you of this arrival for whatever it is worth. One of my servants will place this message in your hands."

I didn't question the truthfulness of this message. Quickly I set my wife and daughter on the road toward Oaxaca. I followed their coach on horseback, escorted by my guard. In less than an hour's time, the Yankee soldiers had entered Tehuacan searching for me. A group of them went to the house where I had been staying, and, finding the door locked, broke it down and searched the rooms with their pistols drawn. General Lanne, the commander of the soldiers, ordered my baggage searched. "The affair of El Pinal has not been avenged!" he shouted.[1]

The third infamous deed involves the famous Benito Juarez. Juarez was the Governor of Oaxaca when I was traveling with my family to that city. He had the barbaric pleasure of denying me refuge and ordered me out of the state.[2] Juarez held a grudge against me from days of old. Once in December, 1828, at the home of Manuel Embides in Oaxaca, he served

117

me a meal when he was dressed in crude cotton trousers and barefooted. I was rather surprised that such a low class Indian would have figured in the history of Mexico.

I am not exaggerating. General Manuel M. Escobar witnessed Juarez's serving me the meal, dressed as I have described. It was not until some time later that a Dominican priest taught Juarez to read and write and to dress in coat, trousers, and shoes.

Like all the guilty, the *ad interim* President, Pena y Pena, suffered from his conscience. Fearing what I might say if he failed to issue me a passport, he granted me one. He also gave me a safe conduct from the invaders with whom he was in league. Pena y Pena, who signed his name to the *Treaty of Guadalupe Hidalgo*,[3] will be forever infamous in the memories of those Mexican patriots of our times.

At last I left my home in the town of Coxcatlan, where I had gone from Oaxaca. Against my wishes, the invading troops formed an echelon for my journey from Perote to Vera Cruz. They arranged for the food for my journey, and insisted on doing me the honor that my position called for.[4] The leaders of the enemy army disapproved of General Lanne's attempted attack on me at Tehuacan. With true feeling, they stated, "General Santa Anna must be respected in his retirement."

In March of 1848, I embarked at the Barra de la Antigua en route to Jamaica. I was cordially welcomed on this English island by the authorities, and

118

I lived there contentedly for two years. However, the language and customs were strange to my family, and they were dissatisfied. In search of a country similar to our own, we moved to Nueva Granada.

In April, 1850, my family and I arrived at the port of Cartagena in Nueva Granada. To get away from the suffocating heat of this walled city, we moved to the town of Turbaco, a few miles away, where the climate was more temperate.

We needed a comfortable house and I rebuilt a ruined house that I purchased for very little money. I was delighted to learn that the illustrious Simon Bolivar, Liberator of Colombia, had lived on my property at one time. Two bronze rings hung in the hall of the house. From these two rings, Bolivar had hung the hammock that he slept in. I took pains to see that these rings were left in their places.

Disgusted and disillusioned with public life and knowing that I would find little peace and contentment in my native country, I resolved to spend the rest of my days in Turbaco. With this resolution in my mind, I began to plan my life. I spent the cool hours of each day beautifying a little country estate, La Rosita, located on the outskirts of town. My family was very happy with the loyal and affectionate friends we made in this charming country. The crypt in which I had planned my last remains to lie still stands in the graveyard there.

In the midst of my tranquillity a Commission from Mexico, composed of Manuel M. Escobar, Salvador

119

Batres, and Doctor Adolfo Hegevich, knocked at my door. They placed in my hands my country's plea for my return to the Presidency. The Commission informed me of the events during the past revolution—events which had caused General Mariano Arista,[5] then head of the government, to lose the confidence of the public.

I was filled with sadness at this call to power. My mind was confused, and the lessons of the past still haunted my memory. I explained to the Commission that I feared the honor they were offering me. However, the pleadings of the Commission were so strong, that I felt it my duty to heed the call of my country. I resolved to abandon my happy retirement and to set out with my family to the port.

Our leavetaking from Turbaco was a sad and melancholy one. The church bells tolled plaintively. The villagers said their "goodbyes" with anguished faces. The sadness of the occasion moved me, but saddest of all was abandoning the little house I had rebuilt with so much care.

It seemed that, as we were leaving, I heard an ominous voice calling to me, "Where are you going, you foolish one?" Ah, the heart never deceives; if only the foolish would listen!

The Autobiography of Santa Anna

Both sides of a letter from Santa Anna "to the Texan Army," attesting to their courage, thanking the Texans for the kind treatment he received, and pledging his friendship in the future. It was written just prior to his release. Courtesy M. H. Loewenstern, Texas Collector.

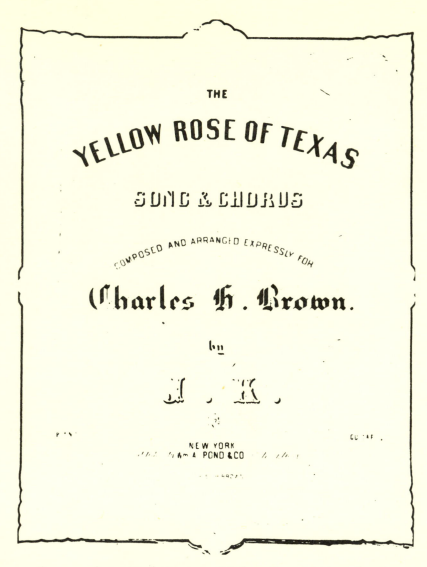

Cover and music of the song, "Yellow Rose of Texas," supposedly inspired by the mulatto girl, Emily Morgan

THE YELLOW ROSE OF TEXAS

GENERAL D. ANTONIO LOPEZ DE SANTA-ANNA.

PRESIDENT OF THE REPUBLIC OF MEXICO.

By A. Hoffy, from an original likeness taken from life at Vera-Cruz.

Portrait of Santa Anna. Commodore E. W. Moore of the Texas Navy attests to its good likeness. C. Dorman David collection.

Lorenzo de Zavala

125

Adrian Woll

GOBIERNO
DE
TAMAULIPAS.

ADRIAN WOLL GENERAL

de Brigada, Benemérito de los Esta-
dos de México y Guanájuato, Goberna-
dor y Comandante general de Tamaulipas à sus habitantes, sabed: que por
el Ministerio de Guerra y Marina se
me ha comunicado el siguiente

Decreto:

El Exmo. Sr. Presidente de la República se ha servido dirijirme el decreto
que sigue.

ANTONIO LOPEZ DE SANTA-ANNA.

*Benemérito de la Patria, General de Division, Caballero Gran Cruz de la Real
y distinguida Orden española de Cárlos III. y Presidente de la República
mexicana,*

A LOS HABITANTES DE ELLA, SABED:

*Que en uso de las facultades que la Nacion se ha servido conferirme, he tenido
á bien decretar la siguiente*

Art. 1.º Se declara vigente la ley de 8 de Abril del corriente año, que some-
tió el delito de robo á la jurisdiccion militar, suprimiéndose en el art. 1.º la es-
cepcion concedida á los reos que sean aprehendidos por fuerza que obre en auxilio
de los jueces ordinarios.

Art. 2.º Los salteadores de caminos que fueren aprehendidos *infraganti*,
y los salteadores que aunque no hayan sido aprehendidos *infraganti*, hayan cau-
sado muerte ó heridas graves en el asalto, serán juzgados en juicio sumarísimo
reducido á la comprobacion del hecho, y se les señala como pena, la capital, que
será ejecutada segun se previene en el art. 6.º

Art. 3.º En ningun caso se admitirá el recurso de indulto para los salteadores de caminos, hayan sido aprehendidos ó no *infraganti*.

Art. 4.º Para dar cumplimiento al art 12 de la espresada ley, en las capita-
les en que residan los comandantes generales, y en cualquiera ciudad, villa ó
pueblo en que hubiere número competente de capitanes, cinco de estos formarán
el consejo de guerra ordinario, para juzgar á los salteadores de caminos, presi-
diendo el mas antiguo de ellos, consultando con auditor ó jueces de lo civil ó criminal donde los hubiere, y donde no, con cualquiera abogado que se halle en el
lugar en que se reuna el consejo, ó en el punto mas inmediato, quedando desde
luego autorizados y obligados por esta ley, á desempeñar este servicio.

Art. 5.º En el juicio sumarísimo mandado establecer para juzgar á los salte-
dores de camino, se nombrará un oficial subalterno, para que verbalmente espon-
ga á favor del reo lo que estimare conveniente.

Art. 6.º En los lugares en que no hubiere el número competente de capitanes
para formar el consejo de guerra ordinario, el comandante principal mas cercano al lugar en que fuere aprehendido el salteador de caminos, será su juez, y consulta-
rá con cualquiera abogado en los términos prevenidos en el art. 4.º, será sub-
balmente á un oficial subalterno que será defensor de oficio, y cuidará de que la
pena sea aplicada irremisiblemente, y cuando mas tarde á las veinte y c.

Presidential decree of Santa Anna, promulgated by General
Adrian Woll.

127

Anastasio Bustamente

Santa Anna's Inauguration in 1845

Pedro de Ampudia

Political cartoon depicting the excesses of Santa Anna's presidency (1845)

Battle of Resaca de La Palma

American troops quartered near Matamoras, 1847

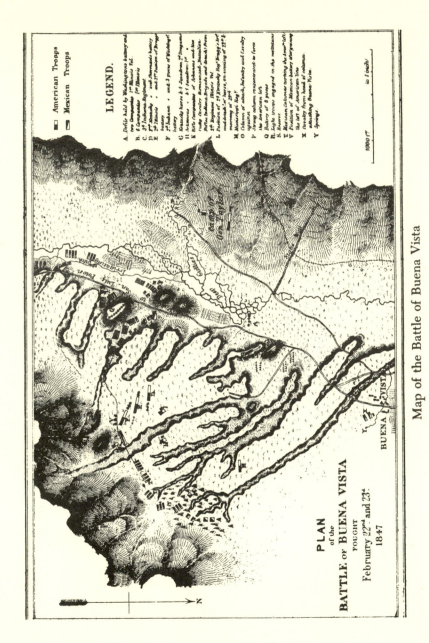

Map of the Battle of Buena Vista

General Zachary Taylor refusing Santa Anna's demand for surrender at the Battle of Buena Vista

General Mariano Paredes

CHAPTER TEN

Revolution—Exile Again (1853-1855)

ON APRIL 29, 1853, General Manuel Lombardini, ever loyal and obliging,[1] placed the power of the government of the Republic once again in my hands.

I chose the most worthy of my countrymen for my Cabinet, and, in order to expedite affairs, I added a Minister of the Interior and a Minister of Public Works. Lucas Alaman was appointed Minister of Foreign Affairs. He was not my friend—a fact he brought to light in his history, *The Revolution in Mexico*.[2] However, I was not looking for men to sing my praises. I chose the most capable men, men who could render valuable service to our nation.

General Juan Alvarez, better known to the people as "The Panther of the South," disapproved of the appointment to the Cabinet of Lucas Alaman. He took the liberty of expressing his disapproval in the following words: "I do not think that Lucas Alaman is worthy of a public position. He was a member of the Cabinet that did away with the highly respected General Guerrero."

I knew that if all of us were to work together for the good of the country, it would be necessary for us to bury forever our past hatreds. When I pointed this out to Alvarez, he attributed my reasoning to fear and replied, "If Alaman continues in the Cabinet, the South will revolt."[3]

From the moment these words were uttered, I would have gladly returned to Turbaco. But honor and duty set my course. I bitterly regretted that fatal hour when I left the peace and tranquility of my retirement. But I recognized my obligations and devoted myself to fulfilling them.

Alvarez openly revolted against my government, gathering about him all those who wished to better themselves through revolt. These traitors set up the *Plan de Ayutla*,[4] using the excuse of my dictatorship for their revolt. They pretended they had never heard Alvarez's congratulations to me on having merited the confidence of the people. They also pretended ignorance of Alvarez's oaths of loyalty—oaths which a man of his class and background could hardly be expected to honor.

Alvarez was a member of the lowest class of Mexicans—direct descendant through his mother of the African race. When he was young he had been a stableboy for General Vicente Guerrero. To Guerrero he owed all the power which he had gained in the mountains of the South. He had practiced cruelties of a savage nature, and the government tolerated him as the lesser of many evils. I, myself, even went so

far as to promote him to the rank of general. To give
you some idea of this wretched man's character, let
me quote you a few lines from the journalist Arbo-
leya's work on Spain and Mexico:

"In both war and peace, man should never
deviate from the truth or risk saying anything
offensive about another person, unless the man
is convinced of the accuracy of the assertion
and has adequate testimony on which to base
it. Knowing this, I am going to acquaint you
with a man who stands out boldly in the picture of the Mexican revolution—a bloody
figure whose grey hairs of old age are stained
by the blood of many cruel sacrifices. These
same grey hairs bristle with lust and wanton-
ness. This is the man to whom the people of
his country have given the nickname,
'Panther of the South.'

"There is a distinct parallel between Rosas,
the tyrant of Buenos Aires, and Juan Alvarez,
the Mexican general who rules as master of
lives and property in the state of Guerrero.
We must note with surprise that the 'Panther
of the South' is the more tyrannical of the two.

"When His Excellency visits his towns, the
simple people receive him on bended knee,
both in the plaza and in the streets. Tears of
apparent tenderness spring into the eyes of that
unmoving tyrant, but soon glances dart out to
find his next victim. A few days later one of his

139

servants announces to the General that his orders have been carried out.

'Did the two die?'

'Your Lordship's wishes have been carried out.'

'Well?'

'Does Your Lordship require anything else?'

'Wait!'

"The General then orders another of his servants: 'Do away with that one, so that he cannot repeat what he has done.' Immediately the double murder, dreamed up between the ovations of the people, is compounded by the death of the paid assassin.

"Who is that naked girl who hangs so horribly from that tree without daring to complain?

"She was unfortunate enough to please 'The Panther,' and he has abused her. Now he has hanged her there so that he may have the pleasure of horsewhipping her every now and then.

"This is frightful and notorious. Such monstrous acts are not invented. And there is only one man capable of committing them. The only consolation that the Spanish-American race can take is that Juan Alvarez is a member of the African race, not of ours."[5] Other similar instances could be cited, but Alva-

rez's character is now well known and I do not wish
to bore the reader. I will only add that no one dared
to contradict Alvarez in his own region. Everyone
submitted to his commands. When he called men for
his revolts, they had to appear before him well armed
and well supplied. Not one of the men was allowed
to draw a salary. When they were wounded in battle,
they were forced to cure themselves, as best they
could. He disposed of public funds at will, and he
did not even know the first principles of waging war.
He proved himself a coward at Molino del Rey, as I
have pointed out. Even then, I kept him from being
judged harshly in a council of war.

At Alvarez's command, the South rose in arms
against the government. As duty commanded, the
government desired to suppress the rebellion at its
source. In order to obtain the quickest and most
effective victory, I took charge of the expedition. I
wished to observe at first hand the notorious mountains of the South, and I led an expedition of four
thousand men armed with mountain guns.

As I advanced, Alvarez lurked in his hideaways
and prepared to receive me at his discretion. If I had
been opposing any other person, I would have been in
danger in the formidable positions of El Coquillo
and El Peregrino. But victory was easy, owing to
Alvarez's ignorance and lack of courage.[6] My troops
surveyed that rugged region as far as Acapulco without once meeting the braggart's army. I sent forces
to pursue him and return to my duties.

141

Alvarez's rebellion would have died at his birth if treachery and ambition had not helped it along. Comonfort, Dagollado, Lallave, and the famous bandit, Pueblita, supported it at the first by promoting the *Plan de Ayutla*. Government troops pursued and defeated them, but, in our explosive country, one spark is enough to set off a forest fire.

Despite the revolution in the South, my government dedicated itself to many reforms in all branches of the administration.[7] Just take a look at them! We very carefully improved all our international relations. The affairs of the many Secretariates were brought together under the regulation of a Council. The administration of the powers of the various governors was facilitated. The Diplomatic Service was established and organized. A public auction was set up to help liquidate the foreign debt we had incurred with France and Spain.

In addition, the legal status of all foreigners in our country was affirmed. We arranged for the administration of justice in all phases of the public tribunals, as well as the tribunals devoted to property and commerce. A bankruptcy law and a penal code relating to revenue officers were established, as was a mercantile code. The business of the admiralty courts was classified, a reform which had been hoped for since the Constitution of 1824.

We managed to separate legal proceedings from those that required a jury, and we set up laws applying to the inviolability of property belonging both to individuals and businesses. We annulled all laws that laid claims on the right to own property, and we did away with all unjust laws relating to subsidies. We formed a general plan of public instruction and organized the universities and colleges of the entire Republic.

Furthermore, we created funds for the judicial department and for public instruction. We regulated the municipalities and listed all public property. We established a police force and passed laws against vagrancy. We set up governmental regulations covering mining and established the first refuse buoys. We opened roads and ferries and provided for their upkeep. We constructed bridges and surveyed rivers. We inspected the railroad running from the capital to the city of Guadalupe Hidalgo and extended the one from Vera Cruz to the interior.

In every one of the decrees and orders issued by the government during my administration, everything that affected the safety of our country—its material advancements, its good, and its glory—was provided for.

The political and financial scene of the Republic presented a very dismal aspect when I took charge of the government in April, 1853. Our neighbors to the north were threatening another invasion if the boundary question was not settled to their satisfaction. Savages and bands of robbers roamed and plundered the countryside. The army had been destroyed and the old military class greatly discouraged. Our political

143

parties were engaged in a fierce struggle, and chaos reigned throughout the nation.

The government under Herrera and Arista had ignored the important Department of the Treasury, and had counted on the fifteen million pesos gainer from the dishonorable and prejudicial *Treaty of Guad alupe Hidalgo*. Also, they had neglected the boundary settlement which, for security's sake, was desperately needed.

The first question to claim my attention was the all-important issue of the boundary dispute with the United States. With knife in hand, the Washington government was attempting to cut another piece from the body which she had just horribly mutilated. We were threatened with yet another invasion. Considering the deplorable condition of our country, I considered a complete break with the United States foolish. I decided to take the alternative which patriotism and prudence decreed—a peaceful settlement.[8]

The Mexican engineers, busily marking the boundaries, stopped their work because of the threatening situation. An American division had already entered the state of Chihuahua, and the Commanding General had sent for orders and reinforcements.

About this time, the Washington government sent Mr. Gaden [James Gadsden][9] to our capital as Minister Extraordinary. He had the necessary powers to settle the boundary dispute once and for all.[10] The fortunate arrival of this envoy from the United States

144

made it possible to enter directly into negotiations. However, several interesting incidents took place in our conferences.

At our first conference, the Mexican Minister of Foreign Affairs was present. The envoy from the United States presented us with a sketch map on which appeared a new boundary—a boundary which gave Baja California, Sonora, Sinaloa, part of Durango, and Chihuahua to the United States. The other half of the territory was left to Mexico. Annoyed by the absurdity of such demands, I threw down the map, exclaiming, "These affairs should not even occupy our time." The envoy withdrew the map and courteously offered not to present it again.

At the second conference, the envoy presented another map. This time the Mesilla Valley was indicated as belonging to the United States. This was highly questionable to us, and we began to discuss the issue. I upheld the opinion of the Mexican engineers that the Mesilla Valley could not belong to the United States. I based the opinion on the fact that the dividing line between the two countries had been well established by the *Treaty of Guadalupe Hidalgo*, and that the Mexican Republic had religiously obeyed the terms of the treaty.

At the next conference, we continued the discussion centering around the Mesilla Valley. The United States Minister grew impatient with the opposition he met and said, "My government will not concede on this question and we are gravely concerned over it.

145

The railroad we intend to build from New York to Alta California must pass through the Mesilla Valley. There is no other feasible route. If the Mexican government will give its consent, we will present Mexico with a generous indemnity."

At another conference, the Minister insisted upon a definite settlement. When I replied that I would think it over, the Minister stated emphatically, "Gentlemen, we will either agree on an indemnity for the Mesilla Valley, or the United States will be forced to take it."

Naturally I became angry at such a remark, but I managed to keep my temper. I knew the situation that my country was in and managed to let my head guide me. I pretended that I had not heard the remark and said to the Minister, "Mr. Gaden, I heard you repeat 'generous indemnity' and I would like to know just how much that might be. I presume that the amount will not be as paltry as that offered for half the Mexican territory."

The Minister was obviously taken aback by the tone of my voice and my manner. For some time he could not find his voice. When he did answer, he choked on his words. "Yes," he stammered, "a generous indemnity."

Our negotiations continued with my saying, "Well, I see that you are definitely in accord with my way of thinking and eager to reach satisfactory terms. I, also, wish to avoid the scandal which would be caused if two neighboring countries were at each other's throats every instant. Just think of the bloody scenes that could be avoided!"

The Minister, with a smile on his face, asked me, "Just what value do you place on the territory of the Mesilla Valley?"

"Oh, let me see," I replied. "In monetary terms, I think that it is worth fifty million pesos."

The surprised Mr. Gaden sprang from his seat, exclaiming, "Fifty million pesos! That's, indeed, a great deal of money!"

"My dear sir," I replied, "when a powerful country wishes to possess that which belongs to another, the powerful country must be willing to pay."

"I'll give you my answer tomorrow," he replied.

On the following day he had his answer for me. "I believe that the best interests of my country lie in making an early settlement of this matter," he said. "Therefore, I am going to use the power my country has granted me and, in its name, offer the Mexican government twenty million pesos to settle the Mesilla Valley question. The United States Treasury will pay ten million pesos on approval of the treaty and the remaining ten million at the end of a year."

I accepted his offer jubilantly. The terms of his proposition greatly exceeded what I had expected, and I could hardly object. Our Minister of Foreign Relations, Manuel Bonilla, immediately began to arrange the terms of the treaty, according to the Minister's wishes. When he finished, it was revised and approved in a council of ministers.

147

THE EAGLE

The Washington government found twenty million pesos to be a good deal of money to pay for the Mesilla Valley. One senator said, "Mr. Gaden has gone out of his mind. I know the territory in question, and I can give you an impartial judgment that it is not worth a fourth of the price they are asking."

After many lengthy debates, the Senate finally approved the treaty, but deducted ten million pesos from the amount stipulated and gave up some of the territory they had asked for.

When my government again considered the boundary question, they gave their consent despite the reduction in price. When they realized that they had obtained a price for a piece of unimproved land that was equal to that obtained for half the National Territory, they realized the need for organized force.[11]

I knew that we must soon begin reorganizing the army, and I exerted a great effort toward beginning this task. We also began repairing the fortresses and gathering equipment for the army. It is a well-known fact that when we had finished our task the army was stronger and more brilliant than ever before. I brought fifty thousand rifles with percussion caps from Cuba and exchanged them for the army's flint rifles. We also brought in cannons for the fortress of Ulua, and we completely reequipped it, as the invaders had left it completely disarmed. We also strengthened the plaza of Vera Cruz and the fortress of Perote.

At that time we had no warships in our ports,

148

and, as I recall, at the time when I left the country in August, 1855, we had eleven steamboats and sailboats. Also, two steam frigates were under construction in Liverpool.

A united army under command of the respected General Adrian Woll protected the northern frontier. The robbers were surpressed, and the roads were once again secure. Count Raoussett B. Boulbon and his adventurers attempted to overpower the port of Guaimas. He was defeated and paid for this rash act with his life. No longer were Mexican nationalism and Mexican dignity empty words. We had a strong army to back them up.

If we did not accomplish more during the short period of my last administration, it was due to the circumstances, not to lack of will. We can only do what is physically possible.

And, nothing was sufficient to bring about peace in our country. Alvarez and his rebels were determined to bring about a revolution. They attempted to cover their plot by crying out against the dictatorship. I considered leaving the dictatorship (which I had not asked for and which I had not wanted) and leaving the country, but my Cabinet was against such a move. I soon gave up the idea.

The arguments of my ministers were well phrased. They said, "The ways of caution are preferable to violence with all its dire consequences. A dictatorship which is set up by the will of the people is not illegal. When such a dictatorship is carried out without abusing the will of the people, and when the interests of the country are forwarded, there is no excuse for attacking it. The President can always appeal to the people who called him to office and gave him his powers. After such a vote, the government will know the will of the people."

These observations seemed quite acceptable to me, and I decided to conform to their justness. When the voting and the returns had been tabulated by the Council,[12] the president of the Council, Luis G. Cuevas, with the Council came to me at the palace. In a solemn ceremony, Cuevas addressed me, "Honored President of the Republic: The Government Council has the honor of being the first to congratulate the Supreme Magistrate on the vote of confidence which the country has given him. This vote of confidence has been given freely and solemnly by the people.

"This vote designates that the President may call a convention to reform the Constitution at his pleasure. The people have also awarded him the title, 'Most Serene Highness.'[13] They have also awarded him the title, 'Captain General,' and a salary of seventy thousand pesos a year. All of these stipulations are stated in these documents, which I have the pleasure of presenting to you."

I was completely mortified by these ridiculous concessions. I forced myself to answer, "Worthy Council! The fact that my conduct in the discharge of my Presidential duties has been accepted by the

150

people is the highest honor that I can attain. Although I appreciate all other honors awarded me and know they are offered sincerely, modesty forces me to reject them. Therefore, I can only answer according to my sentiments. As the title of 'Most Serene Highness' is appropriate to the office of President, I shall only use it in discharging my Presidential duties. The title of 'Captain General' I must renounce, in favor of the medals awarded me on the banks of the Panuco.

"As to an increase in salary, all I have to say is that the President covers all his needs with the twenty-six thousand pesos already allotted to him. It is quite unnecessary to burden the exhausted Public Treasury."

Such confidence and kindness obliged me to continue in my governmental duties and with a zeal that the reforms of my administration reflect. I would have continued to instigate further reforms to the end of my term, if I had continued to have the moral and material support of those near me. But, unfortunately, they chose to join with those who clamored for an early call of the Convention. They added further flame to the fire by their stupid actions in attacking the church, and especially the convent of San Augustine.

The Government Council was composed of forty members of the social elite of the country. I considered their opinion of importance and attended their sessions, accompanied by my ministers. With the greatest displeasure, I learned that all the Coun-

151

cil, with the exception of three members, were in favor of an early call of the Convention. As if it were possible to hold an election with a revolution staring us in the face!

This disagreement between the Council and the government found me in the middle. It seemed that all the men had suddenly lost their common sense! I felt that they were trying to bring about my political death, and I knew that I was only aggravating the situation. In order to free myself from all blame for what was to come, I decided to choose the course of reason and judgment. I decided to resign my office before I was forced to the extreme action of calling for a show of arms to protect my office and person. Such an act would have resulted in nothing good for the country.

Without seeming vain and with due respect to my fellow men, I truly believed that there was no one who could adequately take my place. The man I felt most qualified was the President of the Supreme Court of Justice, Ignacio Pavan, and I delegated my duties to him.[14]

On August 11, 1855, I once more sailed from the port of Vera Cruz, this time on the national steamer *El Guerrero* towed by the *Iturbide*.

CHAPTER ELEVEN

My Exile—Juarez's Rise to Power
(1855-1859)

WHEN I left Mexico once again, ambitious men and anarchists again took hope. The entire country was in confusion; it lacked a powerful leader who could master such a situation. Although he seemed an honorable man, Pavon lacked courage and relinquished his authority to General Martin Carrera.[1] Carrera was pledged to uphold the revolution and had taken advantage of the country's instability. He represented the interests of the South when he came to take possession of the Presidency. Fourteen thousand veterans under the command of General Romulo Diaz de la Vega witnessed his taking of the office.

In the midst of the revolutionary flurry, one could hear harsh voices crying, "The tyrant has fled!" But, more modest ones among the fickle populace moaned, "He has abandoned us!" Every mind in Mexico was filled with the giddiness of revolution.

When Juan Alvarez again gained power, he spent much of his time avenging his defeats at Coquillo and El Peregrino. Without the smallest respect for my many public acts, he ordered my name erased from the army register. Mine was the oldest name on record there. Again, without the slightest respect for the laws regarding private property, he openly confiscated mine as if it were the booty of war. He also claimed my possessions, declaring that they were to be disposed of by the Supreme Court of Justice. No word of this scandalous action reached me.[2]

Juan Alvarez was afraid of power and the position that he held. He knew that many of the people regarded him as an object of ridicule, and many were horrified of him. He found safety only in his caves, and he retired from office. He handed the government of the country over to his favorite, Ignacio Comonfort, the administrator of the customs house at Acapulco and Alvarez's Minister of War. The powerful men of Alvarez's party congratulated themselves on being rid of his disgraceful presence.[3]

Comonfort was well known to me. In 1847, he was determined to gain the auditorship of the customs house at Acapulco, a position that was then vacant. He pled so with me for the position that I gave it to him. In 1853, he again begged for the administratorship of the customs house, having vacated the position some time before. Again I granted him the position he desired. At that time, he could not find words enough to extol my name; but, a few years later, when vanity had overtaken him, he changed these compliments to reproaches.

Comonfort committed even more sacreligious acts.

154

In order to gain favor with his party and to further his ambition, he circulated scandalous rumors about me. He intimated that I had appropriated the money from the sale of the Mesilla Valley, thus making a mockery of the boundary treaty. Power and good fortune make bold a man of low origin and improper sentiment. No other reason could have caused Comonfort to make such statements.[4]

Comonfort terminated the negotiations for the collection of the remainder of the ten million pesos before the date when the payment was due. This caused a scandalous loss to the country's Public Treasury. But in the days of terror and confusion throughout the country, no one dared to contradict him.

Comonfort soon revealed the treachery which was harboring in his breast. He swore an oath to uphold the Constitution of 1857. Immediately afterward, however, he attempted to abolish the Constitution, claiming that it was impossible to govern by it. This act caused Comonfort to lose the office of President, and he fled the country.[5]

Benito Juarez, President of the Supreme Court of Justice, took over for Comonfort. Juarez, having taken advantage of the upheaval brought about by the Revolution of Ayutla, had obtained the Presidency of the Supreme Court of Justice by service to the revolution. The fighting continued against Juarez and the Constitution. Felix Zuloaga and Miguel Miramon both ascended to the Presidency.[6] During the admin-

155

istration of Miramon, my property was once again restored to me, giving me the right to sue for damages against those who had confiscated it. But, as soon as Benito Juarez was once again in power, my property was again confiscated. My children contended in vain for their property rights, claiming that their father had never been in debt to the Public Treasury or to any person.

On learning of the rumors that Comonfort was spreading about me, I contradicted them in a *Manifesto* issued from San Tomas, April 1, 1857. Duty called me to take this action, and I shall repeat my refutation in these *Memoirs*, so as, once and for all, to get the matter straight. Truth needs no explanation; it always triumphs over falsehood.

In 1848 the Public Treasury owed me the sum of two hundred thirty-two thousand pesos for salary and loans I had made to it. Although a law had been passed, calling for the settlement of those sums paid by me for the weapons of war, the settlement went to the credit of the government. Both Herrera and Arista, his successor, ordered that my deficit should continue to the credit of the government.

In 1853, the Secretary of the Treasury, Olazagarri, ordered that the deficit should be paid to me. In the early part of the following year it was paid to Manuel Escandon, who had my authority to collect the sum. This is the payment to which Comonfort alluded in his unwarranted accusations.

As proof that man's conscience often makes up for

his evil deeds, let's take a look at Comonfort's later acts. When he was in exile, he repented of his accusations and evil deeds against me. When he returned to the country, he told my good friend Ignacio Sierra y Rosso to tell me that he was soon to vindicate me through the press. Comonfort was involved in this work when death overtook him.

But my political enemies had seized on the evil words of Comonfort. They hastened to use his slander by such remarks as: "The tyrant has placed forty million pesos in the Bank of London." The easily-swayed population and the press circulated the rumor: "General Santa Anna possesses a colossal fortune."

Slander is like a taste of garlic. Its smell is difficult to erase. How right Machiavelli was when he said, "Slander, slander—it always leaves something behind!"

I was unable to check the exaggerated stories of my wealth, and everywhere that I went I was besieged by businessmen soliciting letters of credit on the Bank of London or asking for donations and loans. I replied to them all: "My dear sir, you are quite mistaken if you believe I have money in the Bank of London. I assure you on my honor that I do not have or have not had a single peso there. My fortune in Mexico consisted of property and my salary. However, as my political enemies have robbed me of both of these, I have nothing. The fabulous fortune which rumor says I have is merely the invention of my enemies, who are attempting to discredit me."

157

THE EAGLE

Despite such a frank explanation, the beggars went away saying, "He has money, but he doesn't want to part with it." I can surely say, without fear of exaggeration, that my enemies would stop at nothing. They scoffed at our country's honor, service to one's country, venerable old age, misfortune—all that the human heart holds dear. But they should know that evil men have never succeeded, and will never succeed, in disturbing the peacefulness of my soul— a soul enlightened by a clear conscience and possessed of a tranquility that will accompany me to my grave.

When I arrived at the port of Cartegena, the good people of Turbaco came to meet me and greeted me with a rousing welcome. The parish priest appeared first, on foot and wet from the falling rain. Then the townspeople cheered me enthusiastically, and the town musicians filled the air with music. Each person vied with the other for the honor of embracing me as I dismounted from my horse. What sweet memories were stirred by the sight of the little house I had left so sorrowfully! How many wonderful memories! Once again I was deserting my country, and with one more disillusionment in my heart.

With my peace of mind once more restored, I returned to my peaceful rural work. Two years and seven months were to pass without even the slightest annoyance to disturb me.

The announcement of an approaching revolution in Mexico once again interrupted my peace of mind. And, once again, this revolution was to bring me new

disasters. In order to escape from the inevitable outcome of such a revolution, I moved to the island of
San Tomas [Saint Thomas] and planned to return
only when the revolution had passed.

The people of Turbaco were sorrowful to find I
truly intended to leave. They petitioned me insistently
to stay. A commission from the townspeople delivered
a written petition to me, which I feel must appear in
this history of my life, as proof of the esteem which
these generous people accorded me.

"Most Excellent Sir, General Antonio Lopez
de Santa Anna:

"It is not for the sake of mere adulation or
personal interest that we take pen in hand to
write a genuine statement to you and to the
entire world. It is the honorable sentiment of
gratitude which guides our hand and a sense
of justice which impels us. In our writing we
shall endeavor not to exaggerate the acts we
shall discuss, and we shall write in the language
which we, sensible and honest men, our hearts
full of gratitude, are accustomed to using.
Therefore, we hope that Your Excellency will
hear us with indulgent attention.

"Since we have learned that Your Excellency has definitely decided to leave us, sorrow
has descended on our town. Our sorrow has
been increased by the fact that our parting
might be forever. We only wish that we could

be inspired with the sweet persuasion of the Apostles and with the sublime eloquence of a Cicero, in order to banish from your mind the thought of leaving us.

"When Your Excellency returned to us in September, 1855, we thought that Divine Providence had sent you to us. We believed it even more, when we heard you say, 'I shall spend the rest of my days among you.' This promise filled us with pride, for we are not ashamed to admit that we are proud to have you as our patron and benefactor.

"But, while we were at peace with this good fortune, we find ourselves faced with a sad and painful farewell—a farewell which fills us with sadness and despair. We have accepted our good fortune on the return of Your Excellency as a gift from Divine Providence for a number of reasons.

"No one can dispute that Your Excellency has been nothing less than a mountain of charity in our community and the surrounding countryside. No one can dispute the fact that everyone—rich and poor, old and young, widow and orphan, shipwrecked sailors and unfortunate convicts—has received kind and generous aid from Your Excellency. Some have been given loans without interest to help relieve their difficulties. Others have received help in bettering themselves and their situa-

160

tion. All have been protected by Your Excellency.

"If we should draw a parallel between Turbaco as it was before Your Excellency arrived and Turbaco as it is now, we should like to point out that our population has doubled. Where there were miserable huts and bare lots in the heart of town, now there are comfortable houses with more improvements every day. Our parochial church, once in complete ruins, has now been restored and the altars completely decorated. Your Excellency provided the ornaments for the altars, and you helped rebuild the curate's house.

"There was no cemetery, and Your Excellency paid to have one built and supplied the materials for an enclosure. We had no industry, with the exception of small cane plantations, which were badly run, and some farming. Today there are more than fifty well-equipped sugar mills. We did not know how to cultivate tobacco or how to breed cattle. Today many families gain their livelihood through these profitable occupations, all introduced by the beneficent hand of Your Excellency. If there are some who have not profited directly from Your Excellency's generosity, they have benefited through the overall improvement of the community.

"All of these great services impose upon us

a duty, and the most sacred duty is one of gratitude. Therefore, because we respect the promise Your Excellency made to us, we humbly beseech you to put off your voyage. We must repeat that we desire Your Excellency to remain with us permanently. We desire your wisdom and esteemed counsel which you so frequently give to us. And Your Excellency's example of steadfastness to an occupation constantly inspires us. As an example to us, you have dedicated yourself to the noble profession of cultivating the soil, not for the profit you might gain from it, but as a means of giving employment to hundreds of indigent citizens. Many of these citizens were in misery before you came, and today many own their own farms.

"As we look on all of these deeds, we can see that Your Excellency's heart is devoted to all that is great, all that is beautiful, all that is heroic, and all that is sublime. If Your Excellency feels that your patriotic duty makes it necessary for you to leave us, then there is nothing for us to do but pray to Almighty God, the Guardian of all human destiny, to protect Your Excellency in your journey and to watch over the citizens of Turbaco, who hold you in their hearts.

"However, if Your Excellency should decide to listen to our pleas and postpone your

162

journey, we would fall on our knees and give thanks to Almighty God for the favor he has granted us."

This petition was dated in Turbaco, February 10, 1858. It was signed by the Mayor, Manuel Tejada, and over one hundred of the townspeople.

CHAPTER TWELVE

Revolution—The French Empire in Mexico (1859-1865)

THE REVOLUTION in Nueva Granada, headed by General Tomas C. de Mosquera, was a long and bloody one. I spent five years in San Tomas[1] waiting for the end of the revolution and for order to be restored. During this time, rumors were circulated about that Europe was looking toward Mexico with the hope of reestablishing an Empire there.[2] Soon the news reached me that the Archduke of Austria, Maximilian of the house of Hapsburg,[3] had been named Emperor of Mexico, under the protection of France, England, and Spain. Maximilian had been sent to Mexico at the request of a Mexican agency.

This news excited me and aroused my curiosity to such a point that I sailed for Mexico in the early part of February, 1864.[4] When the English packet boat, on which I was sailing, docked at the port of Vera Cruz, a French Colonel, calling himself "Governor of the Plaza," appeared on deck with his secretary and an aide. In our interview, the following conversation took place:

"General, will you kindly inform me what the purpose of your visit to this country is?" the Colonel asked.

"There is nothing improper in my visit," I replied. "I am merely returning to my country to enjoy the right that every man has of living where he was born."

"That is quite in order," he answered, "but you must swear an oath of loyalty to the Empire and to the Emperor."

"To what Empire and to what Emperor do you refer?" I asked.

"What!" he exclaimed. "Haven't you heard that the Archduke Maximilian has been called to Mexico and has been recognized by the Mexicans as their Emperor? Why, three great European powers are behind him!"[5]

"I have heard something," I replied. "And, now that I am in the country, I hope to become better informed. However, at the present time, my wife is extremely nauseated, and her condition preoccupies me. I would like to disembark as soon as possible. As to my plans, I assure you that I shall always uphold the laws and the will of the nation."

"Well, then," he said, "sign your name in this book."

His secretary presented the book to me, and I signed my name. The newspapers of Mexico announced my return to the country with this comment, "He has recognized the Empire."

The Regency had been duly established, and as

duty demanded, I presented myself before the established government and announced my arrival. General Bazaine, commander-in-chief of the French army, took offense because I failed to pay my respects to him. Taking advantage of power he did not have, he ordered me expelled from the country.[6] A French steam frigate conducted me to Havana.

I waited there for two months before I learned of the dissolution of the Triple Alliance, the reembarcation of the Spanish army, and the splendid reception in the capital for Archduke Maximilian. He was recognized as Emperor throughout our Republic, now converted into an Empire under the protection of France.

I considered the French Marshal's conduct to me both unusual and scandalous and informed his government of it. I requested satisfaction from them for his conduct. The Emperor Napoleon was kind enough to write me a letter, informing me that he was extremely annoyed by Marshal Bazaine's conduct toward me. As to my petition, he informed me that he would pass it on to the Mexican Emperor for any judgment he would deem fitting. I never heard from my petition again.

Archduke Maximilian, titular Emperor of Mexico, did not seem to think that I merited the consideration of being invited to return to my native soil. My friends wrote to me: "The Imperialists will never have confidence in you. They remember only too well that you destroyed the throne of Iturbide and proclaimed the Republic." At last, I was convinced that I would not be called again to aid my country, and I sailed once more for San Tomas.[7]

The first reports that I received from Mexico were favorable to the Empire. They stated:

"The entire country recognizes and obeys the Emperor. There is both money and enthusiasm throughout the country. Maximilian is visiting the towns in the interior of the country, and everywhere he is greeted with enthusiastic ovations. . . ."

Later reports, however, showed a somewhat different feeling:

"The Emperor and General Bazaine appear not to be getting along so well. The French display a stern character, and military commissions are shooting Mexicans in large numbers. They seem to think that they are in Algiers. Conditions are changing, discontent is becoming more generalized throughout the country, and we are definitely headed for trouble."

The last reports were desperate:

"The situation is becoming more intolerable every moment. We need a strong leader, capable of beginning and ending a movement against these foreigners, if we Mexicans are to ever prosper again."

There was no doubt that the Mexican people were discontented with the French rule. In order to tell them that I was in complete sympathy with them and to give them my support, I wrote and published the *Manifesto* of July 8, 1865.[8] This *Manifesto* was extremely influential wherever it was read and helped to bring about the revolution which followed.

¡VIVA EL GENERAL SANTA-ANNA!

Con repiques y con diana
Y salvas de artillería,
Brilla en México alegría:
Gritabas ¡Viva SANTA-ANNA!

¡Qué regocijo se vió!
¡Qué plácemes de victoria!
El pueblo con grande gloria
Su desembarque aplaudió,
Con voluntad victorió
La venida de Santa-Anna.
A la una de la mañana
Iban á la ciudadela:
No mas bcian la humareda
Con repiques y con diana.

¡A qué fuego tan granbeado
Se vió por los batallones
De fusiles y cañones,
De cohetes acompañado!
Nadie se encontró asustado
Pues hoy se ha llegado el dia
Que todos con alegría
Aguardan al presidente,
Desde el pobre hasta el decente
Con salvas de artillería.

¡Qué bien aplaudió el noveno
Y la guardia nacional
La voz era general
Que viva por siglo eterno!
Un benemérito bueno
Que al tejano le canela
Quitará la balentía
Porque es gránde su valor
Hoy se molerá Tailor
Brilló en México alegría.

¡Mexicanos! el amor
Con que gritamos contentos,
Vámonos á pasos lentos
Y verán á un gran señor,
Esto viene á ser favor
A la Nación Mexicana,
De hacer libre y soberana
Y ponernos en quietud,
Esta es su solicitud;
Gritemos ¡Viva SANTA-ANNA!

RINCONADA DE SANTA CATARINA MARTIR NUM. 3.

A patriotic poem extolling Santa Anna's leadership during the Mexican War. C. Dorman David collection.

Battle of Cerro Gordo

170

Storming of Molino del Rey

American troops attacking Chapultepec

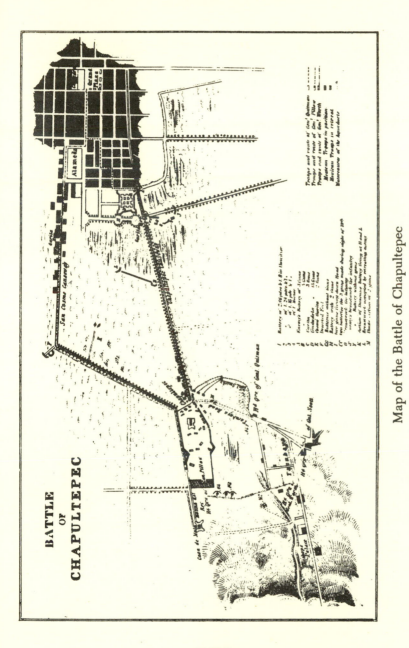

Map of the Battle of Chapultepec

Mariano Arista

174

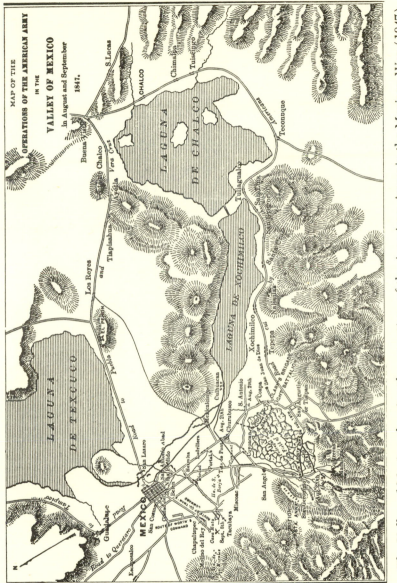

The Valley of Mexico, showing the operations of the American Army in the Mexican War (1847)

175

Santa Anna in uniform

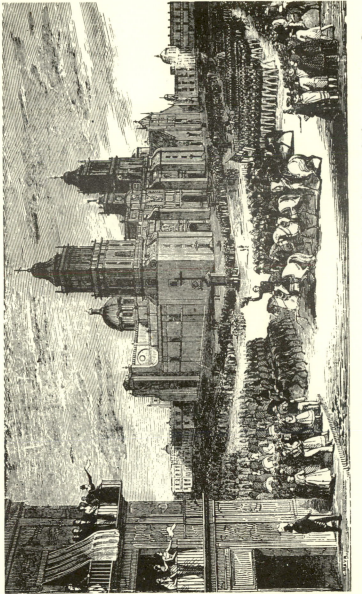

General Winfield Scott and his army entering victoriously into the Grand Plaza at Mexico City

Valentin Canalizo

Campeche

179

Miguel Barragan

Santa Anna as President of Mexico

Nicolas Bravo

182

A political cartoon, depicting Santa Anna's final return from exile. Santa Anna is pictured carrying his gamecocks on his back.

Juan N. Almonte

CHAPTER THIRTEEN

Mr. Seward—The Infamous Plot Against Me (1865-1866)

THE UNITED STATES newspapers spoke out strongly against the French remaining permanently in Mexico. This fitted in well with my plans, and I thought that I might look to the United States for help in heading a movement to drive the French from my beloved homeland. My enthusiasm was so great that I wrote to the President of the United States, asking him to aid me directly or indirectly.

I was beginning to despair of ever receiving a reply to my request when a United States man-of-war dropped anchor in the port of San Tomas. The United States Secretary of State, William H. Seward, was on the vessel, and he presented himself at my home immediately upon leaving the Governor's residence. Mr. Seward's visit was entirely unexpected, and I was extremely curious to know what he had in mind.

After half an hour's conversation with him I was no closer to this objective, as his words were uttered in such a low voice. He constantly spoke as if he wished to speak out, but always checked himself.

He wanted to know why I had journeyed to Vera Cruz when the town was occupied by the French, and I gave him my answer.

From the diplomat's mysterious conduct, I clearly understood his motives. We were in complete agreement on the matter of expelling the French from Mexico, and he was offering me his protection. On leaving my home, he took my hand and grasped it securely. Looking me straight in the eye, he said, "General—to Mexico!" The following day I was going to pay Mr. Seward a visit, when his ship weighed anchor and sailed.[1]

This unusual and sudden appearance of the United States Secretary of State in San Tomas gave the curious something to talk about. They suspected that plans were afoot, and they remembered the gigantic feast the captain of an American ship had given me a few days before.

Now I must introduce you to a gigantic scoundrel, one Dario Mazuera of Nueva Granada, the instigator of the infamous plot which was to take me to the United States and to rob me of a fortune. I must describe this man to you in detail, as he plays such a large part in the misfortunes which were to befall me.

Although only twenty-six years old, Dario Mazuera found it easy to carve a niche for himself among high society. He cut an elegant figure and had the facility for making small talk. Restless and bold by nature, he made himself notorious for savage ferocity, when he joined the ranks against General Mosquera in the Nueva Granada revolution. Fleeing from Mosquera, he took refuge in Peru.

From Peru, he wrote me two letters, asking me to send him autobiographical facts, so that he might begin writing the story of my life. He stated that he had a decided interest in me, although we had never met.

Such an interest seemed rather strange to me, and I replied to him giving him no more facts than courtesy demanded. After the revolution and fall of the President of Peru, Mazuera appeared in San Tomas. He had gathered a small fortune from his benefactor by betraying him.

One night, when he seemed strangely tired, he said to me, "I have spent all day getting ready for my trip to New York, and I have not been able to see you before now. I shall be sailing early tomorrow morning. From New York, I shall be going to Washington, and it would give me pleasure if I could be of service to you while I am there. I have no need of money."

He showed me his pocketbook stuffed with bank notes. It seemed to me a good chance to send a letter to the President of the United States, and I gave my letter to Mazuera, telling him how important the letter was. From Washington, he wrote, "I have had a good journey and have seen the President. I delivered your letter to him. As these men greatly economize in their use of words, he gave me no reply."

187

His second letter stated, "I presented myself to the Secretary of State, Mr. Seward, as your friend and agent. He received me most courteously."

In his third letter, he merely reported that the Secretary of State was out of the city and that he had not seen him again. Mr. Seward's trip to San Tomas fitted in with Mazuera's schemes perfectly. In his fourth letter, he said, "The Secretary of State has returned from his trip and is in a most happy mood. You cannot imagine how satisfied he was after talking with you. He seems to like you very much, and has told me that I might see him at my convenience."

Mazuera's last letter from Washington stated, "I have succeeded in gaining the confidence of Mr. Seward. I gave a dinner party for him and had the satisfaction of seating him on my right and of seating an influential senator on my left. I hope soon to be with you, if all goes well." He even wrote further from New York, "I am now in route to San Tomas but am stopping over here for three days. I hope to obtain information from General Ortega and other Mexican liberals who have fled here from the Empire. I am determined to get them to think favorably of you, as they can be of great help to you against the French. I hope to have news for you when I am there."

Mazuera was merely scoffing at the good faith I had placed in him, while I believed that I had found in this evil man the help I so desperately needed.

188

When Mazuera finally arrived in New York, he was accompanied by Abraham Baez, Vicente Julve, and Luis de Vidal y Rivas. He came to see me immediately, and stated, "General, we have come for you. You are expected in New York, and when we arrive, cannons from the fortress will salute the most illustrious Mexican general. In order that your trip should not be detailed, I have purchased the fast and beautiful steamer, *Georgia*, for a sum of two hundred fifty thousand pesos. You can see it now in the bay."

The purchase of a ship of such enormous value seemed foolish to me, and I refused to approve its purchase. But Mazuera was a man of resources, and he continued unperturbed in his work. He brought me a letter from my friend, the distinguished Venezuelan General Jose A. Paez.[2] The letter stated:

"I take great pleasure in giving you my opinion on the undertaking you have decided on. Such an undertaking is worthy of an illustrious patriot, who is rightly incensed to see his native land dominated by foreigners, who, without mercy, shed the blood of his fellow countrymen. You will be able to find the resources you need in this rich country that advocates freedom. The time is ripe for you to come, and you will afford me the pleasure of seeing you."

The next day Mazuera and his traveling com-

189

panions met at my home. The Peruvian Consul, Miguel Lozano, accompanied them. Mazuera presented me with a paper bearing a large seal. The contents were written in English and translated into Spanish. Mazuera stated solemnly, "The Honorable Mr. William H. Seward, Secretary of State in Washington, was kind enough to give me this memorandum with the request that I place it personally in your hands. I have the pleasure of so doing. Senor Miguel Lozano, a faithful friend, has been kind enough to translate it into Castilian. I think that its contents will show whether or not my heroic efforts on behalf of the General have paid off."

When everyone was seated, I asked the translator to read the message. He read the following in a very loud voice:

"Confidential Memorandum
"A loan of fifty million pesos has been granted to Mexico by the House of Representatives. I am sure that it will have the same results in the Senate. Thirty million of that sum may be used for the expedition of General Santa Anna. It is most necessary that he be here, and he will receive this aid.
Washington, April 2, 1866   Seward"

I couldn't hide my pleasure at this unexpected memorandum, nor did I think to examine its authenticity. I only asked one question of Mazuera: "Mr.

Seward gave you this memorandum personally?" I watched him intently.

"Yes, sir," he replied. "He presented it to me in the Cabinet room."

There is nothing easier than fooling a man of good faith, a man who is not capable of thinking evil of anyone. And, so I fell into their trap. I told the entire gathering, "If the contents of this document are to be valued by us, then there is nothing left to do but get ready to leave."

Mazuera observed my movements without batting an eyelid. He took advantage of my eagerness to place before me the notes for the steamer, *Georgia*. These notes had been taken over from Baez, a cunning Jew who had earned the nickname, "Merchant of New York." They were collectable two months from that date.

How could I refuse a man who had shown himself to be worthy of my confidence? In order to waylay any difficulty, I had to accept the responsibility. I signed the notes. Then, Baez played his part well. With a remorseful smile, he informed me he had promised to deliver forty thousand pesos to the captain of the *Georgia*. He said if he failed to do so, he would suffer a heavy fine. I did not have that much money, but I knew that I had to help him. The money was found and I accepted the responsibility for its repayment.

CHAPTER FOURTEEN

My Trip to New York—
Further Infamies (1866-1867)

TWO DAYS LATER, May 6, 1866, I set sail on the steamer *Georgia* for New York. Accompanying me were my son, Angel, a secretary, Miguel Lozano, Colonel N. Almada, Mazuera, Baez, Julve, Vidal y Rivas, and a recorder, Manuel Mesa. On the eighth day, we arrived in New York. There was no reception in the port, as Mazuera had told me there would be.[1] This made me somewhat uneasy. Baez conducted me to his house in Elizabeth Port,[2] in order that the traitors might have me under their thumbs.

Mazuera, Baez, and Vidal y Rivas set out to Washington to inform Seward of my arrival in the country. However, the commission returned without being received by the Secretary of State. Vidal y Rivas, an honorable man not connected with the plot, remarked to me that, as he saw it, the situation looked like infamy on the part of Mazuera and the others.

Many curious people came to visit me during my stay in New York. Among these was a friend of Mr. Seward's, one Jorge Y. Trunovoll, a good-natured, wealthy man. Knowing that I might communicate with Seward through him, I returned his visit and requested a conference with him. I told him what had been happening, and he offered to go to Washington to find out information for me.

When Mr. Trunovoll returned from Washington, he told me, "The Secretary of State was quite surprised when I told him of the events you described. He says that he has never seen Dario Mazuera, and that he has never been in conference with him. He says that he is occupied now with the Count of Montholon, Envoy Extraordinary from the Emperor Napoleon, in matters pertaining to Mexico. With the Envoy before him, he cannot receive General Santa Anna, and said that it would be best if you would contact the French."[3]

I was stunned by the news. There was no doubt that Mazuera was deceiving me, and that I had been the willing victim of his shameless plotting. What should I do now? At first, I thought of returning immediately to San Tomas. But I was waiting for a reply from President Juarez to whom I had offered my sword in all sincerity, offering to help liberate the Mexican people from their French oppressors. I resolved to wait.

I had Baez rent me a furnished house in New York. The rent for a four months' period was two thousand four hundred pesos—a scandalous rent, which I agreed to rather than living with the accomplice of Mazuera. I could not endure the sight of him.

193

THE EAGLE

After I moved to New York, two men informed me that the steamer *Georgia* belonged to the firm they represented. Abraham Baez had chartered the ship to conduct passengers and merchandise to San Tomas. He had paid ten thousand pesos for this privilege, and the men had informed the captain that if Baez wanted to buy the ship, he might. When Baez had arrived in New York, he had paid eight thousand pesos in notes as a down payment on the ship. Baez had signed my name to the notes, and the men had informed him that the ship would not be delivered until the money was paid in gold coin. Their story completely exposed Baez and left no doubt that he was one of the plotters against me.

Juarez took advantage of the situation to completely rebuff my kind offer. His Minister of Foreign Relations, Sebastian Lerdo de Tejada, brought me a letter that seemed more an insult than an official communication from a government which recognizes and respects dignity. Although I knew Juarez wished me no good, I was surprised by such a rude answer— almost an insult to me—when his country was in danger and everyone was turning against him.

Soon another sad event added to my misfortunes. My secretary, Miguel Lozano, died just at the time when I needed him most. When I asked Lozano about his strange illness, he told me, "I was invited to breakfast by Julve and Mazuera. I felt a most peculiar pain in my stomach, and, as it continued, I hailed a carriage and returned here. I felt like I had been

194

poisoned, and I asked Colonel Almada to give me, in quite small doses, the poison antidote which I have carried for years should such an occasion arise. However, it has had no effect. Perhaps I waited too long to take it. I feel very ill . . . ."

When I returned to see him the next day, he was quite restless. He has passed a bad night, and, on seeing me, he made a great effort to speak. "My dear General," he said, "I am dying. They poisoned me at breakfast . . . they feared I might talk and are getting rid of me. Take care! Oh, my poor family! My poor unfortunate family is in San Tomas without support! I trust them to your well-known generosity!"

He couldn't speak another word. The death rattle in his throat cut off his speech. Although he said no more, no one doubted that Mazuera had poisoned him. Lozano knew about the forged document and had told Mazuera so. Mazuera had killed him to keep him from speaking.

While all these unfortunate events were taking place, the note that I had signed in San Tomas came due. I was growing more confused every day, as I was short of money and unfamiliar with the laws of the United States. It seemed to me that the best move would be to call in the notes and nullify them as soon as possible. I was afraid of serious consequences if I did not do so, and I had to use Julve, as I had not seen Mazuera since he had returned from Washington. He was undoubtedly afraid of my accusing him of the traitorous plot.

Julve got notes for one hundred seventy thousand pesos from Mazuera at a cost of four thousand pesos in gold and the promise not to reclaim the forty thousand pesos which Baez had received in San Tomas. The remaining eighty thousand had been paid to Williams and Company in payment for the *Georgia*. Although the heads of Williams and Company were informed of the plot against me, these men, taking advantage of my difficulties, were audacious enough to ask me for twenty-five thousand pesos. I had to satisfy their greed and knew the money would be less than the cost of a lawsuit. To keep my good name, I gave them my promissory note for the twenty-five thousand pesos.

Until the note could be paid, I handed over to them a small chest of jewels, containing valuables worth more than thirty thousand pesos. These jewels still remain in the possession of these greedy, conscienceless men, as my wretched position made redeeming them impossible. Such were the sacrifices that I had to make to clear my name, linked with the perfidious schemes of Mazuera and Baez.

When we had been aboard ship, Baez had arranged for me to stay at his home. On the day following my arrival in Elizabeth Port and while I still trusted Baez, I gave him ten thousand pesos in gold for him to exchange into paper money for my convenience. Greedy at the sight of so much gold, Baez appropriated the entire sum. To cover his robbery, he said that it cost him a hundred pesos to feed me each day. I confessed that, at that moment, I blushed for having accepted a Jew's hospitality. I finally consented to let him keep five thousand pesos to compensate for the expenses I had incurred during my three weeks' stay. Needless to say, this was far more than was owing.

I was much mistaken if I had ever thought that Mazuera was avoiding me through fear or shame for his deeds. He carefully observed my actions, and, since I was not pursuing him, he continued to rob me of everything that he could. This audacious and evil man made up a story about purchasing some rifles for over one hundred thousand pesos. A commercial house, in league with Mazuera, demanded payment. Now it was absolutely necessary to take the offensive. I hired a lawyer, Daly, to take my case before a court of justice, sparing nothing in my defense and establishing my rights.

Mazuera, no doubt picturing himself inside prison walls, became intimidated and confessed that, indeed, there had been no such rifles purchased and admitted that he had deceived me. The court proceedings ceased, and, when Mazuera presented his papers showing that he was my confidential agent, he was allowed to go free. I only agreed to cease the proceedings because my lawyer was collecting the enormous fee of thirty thousand pesos.

But Mazuera, who had managed to evade man's justice, failed to evade—indeed, who does?—Divine justice. He met the untimely end that so often befalls

197

a criminal. In February, 1869, he was shot as an armed conspirator—guilty or not—at Merida in Yucatan. He finally suffered the death that he so richly deserved.

When winter arrived, I was still in New York. I accepted the invitation of a Hungarian I had befriended in Mexico to spend some time on Staten Island. It is difficult to set down on paper the events which occurred during my unfortunate stay there. He, with some other businessmen, deceived and robbed me, even leaving me without food.

I cannot, even now, recall my stay in New York without bitterness. How I regretted Mr. Seward's visit to San Tomas—that fateful first step in the plot to ruin me. If it had not been for Seward's visit, Mazuera would never have deceived me. I would have examined the false memorandum more closely and thrown it aside. Or Mazuera would have not had the audacity to invent the plot, and I would never have taken that fateful trip, which cost me all—even my life.

CHAPTER FIFTEEN

Back to Vera Cruz—
Imprisonment (1867)

I LEFT NEW YORK on May 6, 1867,[1] accompanied by Luis de Vidal y Rivas. I sailed on the steamer *Virginia* of the Vera Cruz, Havana, and Sisal trade lines bound for Havana and San Tomas. In six days we arrived in Vera Cruz, where the ship was detained in order to unload flour. Friends and acquaintances visited me on board and informed me of the situation in the country. A force under the command of the young General Benavides was besieging the town. The garrison was commanded by two thousand foreigners and nationalists faithful to the Emperor Maximilian. Maximilian had been betrayed in Queretaro and delivered over to the Republicans. The capital continued faithful to the Empire, supported by a garrison of six thousand men under the command of General Tabera.

The first visitors I received aboard ship were the Imperial Commissary, Domingo Bureau, and the Commander of the Plaza, Antonio Taboada. They seemed to be vacillating between the sides they wished to support in the struggle, and I advised them to spare themselves a humiliating surrender and proclaim the Republic. I offered to be present when they proclaimed the Republic, as I had proclaimed or founded the Republic at this same place forty-five years before. My counsel seemed to please them, and they offered to canvass the garrison to find out the opinion there.

I spent one day at the Fortress of Ulua with the commander, General Perez Gomez. Gomez honored me at a small dinner, repaying the favors which I had granted him in Mexico. This quite harmless and social occasion, together with some "Vivas" delivered by the people of the garrison when they saw me, alarmed the visionaries. They even spread the rumor that I had rebelled with the fortress.

Bureau and Taboada informed me that there were too many differing opinions within the garrison and that their conference had been without results. However, when Bureau turned aside to talk to someone else, Taboada said to me, "Bureau is rich and is only thinking of saving himself. He definitely wishes to surrender the town without any reservations. It is absolutely necessary that you come on shore. Your presence and the authority that you hold will help prevent an unconditional surrender."[2]

I swore on my honor that I would be on shore by five in the afternoon and to help support the Republic. I was totally occupied with Mexican affairs: Maximilian had been thrown into prison in Queretaro.

200

This sad young prince, flattered by the commission of Mexicans who had appealed to him and brought him to their country, had been received in Mexico with cheers and hurrahs. His qualities and good works allowed him to reign as Emperor for some time without any disturbances. He had many followers who served the Empire faithfully.

Maximilian had faith in the nobility of the Mexicans with their many promises of working together. He stood true to his honor and the promises he had made to the Mexican people, and he refused to leave the country with the French. I told myself that, considering all his good deeds, no one would dare make an attempt against his life.

To uphold my country's honor, I would gladly have appealed to Benito Juarez to spare his life and allow him to return in peace to his home in Miramar and to his wife. But, what weight would my entreaties have carried? Most likely they would only serve to further harm him! In the end, Juarez was determined to see the Prince dead, and, I, one of his defenders, could do nothing to rescue him. Juarez was dedicated to bloodshed, and many met their fate on the gallows in those days of terror.

I intended to keep my word to Taborada, and I stood on the prow of the *Virginia*, waiting for the time to come to land. Suddenly an officer, very tall and with an exceedingly evil face, appeared on board asking for General Santa Anna. The captain brought him to me, and I, mistaking him for one of the many visitors who came to see me, rose and offered him a chair.

"I have not come for a social visit," he replied roughly. "I have come to remove you to my ship. I am the commander of the United States man-of-war *Tacony*."[3] I knew immediately that I was in the presence of the enemy.

"Oh, God," I exclaimed in surprise, "the United States is declaring war on Mexico again! Did you come to take me into custody as a prisoner of war? I have no soldiers, and I am not prepared to defend myself. I hope that you do not plan to use force on an undefended man."

The commander merely replied, "I have no time to bother with explanations. If you won't come peacefully, we shall take you by force."

A kindly German passenger, who had served as my interpreter on board ship, saw four soldiers from the *Tacony* making their way toward me. He came toward me and said, "General, let us spare you any insult. Give me your arm and I shall help you go aboard the American ship. I think the American commander has evil intentions toward you."

I realized that he was right, and we sailed toward the *Tacony*, anchored off the Island of Sacrificios, and went aboard without saying a word. The commander led me to his cabin, saying, "There you have a bed to lie on, and these servants to supply you with whatever you might need." He indicated his own bed and two young boys who were waiting there.

"Thank you," I replied, "but I shall need nothing. I am endeavoring to find out if I am a prisoner of war and why I am being treated in this manner."

"You were not safe in Vera Cruz," he answered. "Your life was in danger."

"And what right have you to interfere in affairs which are best left to Mexicans?" I demanded.

The commander rose from his chair, saluted me, and said merely, "Good night." He took two steps and then turned and said to me, "I have been an admirer of General Santa Anna's for a long time. It gives me great pleasure to have saved his life." Then he turned away. My German friend interpreted the conversation between us.

The two servants brought me food and ice water, but I neither ate nor drank. The commander's last words disturbed me profoundly, and I spent the night sleepless in my arm chair. Who in Vera Cruz could possibly wish to see me dead?

The next morning at seven an officer told me that the steamer *Virginia* was waiting alongside of us and that I was free to transfer to her if I wished. As I left the ship, the commander shook my hand and said, "Goodbye, General. It has been a pleasure to save your life."

Three days later the *Virginia* was anchored in sight of the port of Sisal. We were detained for three days while the *Virginia* boarded cargo and passengers bound for Havana.

We learned that in the city of Merida, a mere ten

leagues from Sisal, the Republicans and the Imperialists were fighting desperately. My human feelings led me to offer services as mediator between the two commanding chiefs, in order to bring about a reconciliation and to spare the blood of my countrymen.[4]

Zepeda Peraza, my longtime enemy, was captain of the Republicans. He had sworn revenge for the fact that my government was in command when local authorities had charged him with inciting a rebellion. Although I had no knowledge of these charges, he believed that they had come from me. Peraza saw his chance to get revenge and took it. He ordered two gun boats, under the command of the Commandant of Sisal, to fire on the steamer *Virginia*, to seize me, and to escort me to land.

The captain of the *Virginia* protested vigorously against having his flag violated and me conducted from the ship.[5] But, nothing could stop these pirates, and Vidal y Rivas, in order to accompany me, declared himself a prisoner also. When we landed, the military commandant made me a virtual prisoner in his house. He told me that he did not agree entirely with his chief; he was a good man and treated me decently. Four days later, I was sent to Campeche, Vidal y Rivas accompanying me.

What a miserable lot my political enemies in Campeche were! The minute I set foot on the shore, they surrounded me with soldiers, as if I were a traitorous rebel. They led me through the main streets, as prisoners of war had been led during the

Middle Ages.⁶ Then they threw me into an encampment and surrounded me with guards. The people witnessed this barbarous spectacle, but they failed to commit the excesses my enemies had tried to provoke them to.

I was allowed no visitors and no food for a day and a half, and I was growing restless and tried to find out the cause of my mistreatment. A Spanish store owner heard of my plight and sent one of his servants to bring me food. I shared the meal with Vidal y Rivas, who was locked in another room.

I was held prisoner for two months and then was transferred to a pilot boat and taken to Vera Cruz, according to Juarez's orders. Four hours before we were to leave, I was surprised by a visit from my beloved wife and her two brothers. It was torture for her to witness my miserable circumstances. How greatly she had suffered during the past months! We could not postpone my sailing to give her time to organize herself, and she left with me just as she was.

While we were traveling to Vera Cruz, my wife told me that she had gone to Juarez with tears in her eyes to beg for permission to accompany me. The mere sight of Juarez sent terror through her, and to her entreaties, Juarez merely replied, "Madam, you will arrive there too late!"

At the port in Vera Cruz, they forced my wife and me to separate, sending me to Ulua, where I was locked up again in the foulest of dungeons. There was not even a bench to sit on, and they provided little food. One of my brothers-in-law brought me a table, two chairs, and a cot. These were the only furnishings I was allowed.

My jailers would have let me starve to death, if they had had their way. However, my son made arrangements to send food both to me and Vidal y Rivas, locked in another cell.

CHAPTER SIXTEEN

My Trial (1867)

DAYS AND WEEKS passed without my knowing what was going to happen to me. I received no communication from the outside world for a month and a half. One day a newly-appointed lieutenant colonel named Alva appeared in my cell and told me arrogantly, "I am here to notify you that I have been named prosecuting attorney to try your case. I shall open legal proceedings against you tomorrow, trying you under the law of January 5, 1862."

"I know of no such law," I answered. "What is this law?"

"The one that the President passed in order to try traitors to his government," Alva told me.

Now I knew what Juarez was planning. I wrote, as best I could, a protest, which I gave the lawyer, hoping that he might use it at my trial. I wish to state it here, just as I wrote it.

"I, Antonio Lopez de Santa Anna, 'General of Division,' 'Benemerito de la Patria,' etc., with right on my side, protest against the violence committed against me when I was forcibly taken from the steamer *Virginia*, sailing under the flag of the United States, en route to my home in San Tomas.

"I also wish to protest against my imprisonment, the cause of which I know not. When I was arrested in Campeche, I was treated abominably, being denied food and the considerations that were owed me, a person who bears the proud titles bestowed by my countrymen.

"I have been notified that tomorrow I shall be tried, according to the law of January 5, 1862. I have no knowledge whatsoever of this law. I know that I have enemies who plot against me, and, having no other means to defend myself, I declare that I shall not recognize this law to be legal. Therefore, knowing that justice is on my side, I protest, now and as many times as are necessary, against any judgment, trial, accusation, sentence, or any other prejudicial, pretentious act of violence committed against me.

"Without putting undue emphasis on the fact that the President is entirely in the wrong in having me tried and in keeping me prisoner for so long a time, I cannot omit, in self-defense, a truthful observation that is evident on first sight. Surely it is not possible that the President has forgotten that in June of last year, I wrote to him, placing myself at his command to help in any way that he might deem fit to aid my fellow countrymen, then dominated by the tyrannical French.

"Although our President was at that time a mere wanderer on the northern frontier, I recognized that he was in charge of the government. I made my offer through his Minister Romero in Washington, and through Romero, he sent me a reply, authorized by his Minister of Foreign Relations Lerdo de Tejada—a reply which seemed to me more an infamous libel or the work of a madman, than the official document of a respected country. These facts the two ministers can testify to.

"My trip to the United States was prompted by no other motive than to find resources for an expedition against the invaders of Mexico. This fact is well known to everyone. In view of these facts, I do not see how anyone can be convinced, as the President is, that I should be tried as a supporter of the Empire.

"If I am forced to undergo a trial, I shall invoke the fundamental law which is in my favor. According to this law, no citizen can be imprisoned for more than twenty-four hours without being informed of why he is being held. Nor can he be judged by special laws or private tribunals. I put my faith in these laws and in the honor and justice inherent in our country. I am confident that on this occasion the majesty of the law will reign supreme over evil. Going through a trial does not displease me, so long as I am convinced that integrity and right will be regarded. For, in this manner, my honor and my life would be respected.

"I would prefer that a competent authority should review my last administration. During this administration, I was granted extensive powers by the will of the people. If such a review were undertaken, my labor and efforts during this administration would be known and esteemed by all, and my defamers would be proven liars.

Dated and signed:

Antonio Lopez de Santa Anna"

The prosecuting attorney read through my protest and said to me, "I shall present this to the court as it is, but I strongly suggest that you, at least, present your declaration and answer any questions that you are asked."

To refuse seemed useless. I was forced to reply to him, "I have been brought here by force. You must use force to get from me what you wish."

The legal proceedings revealed what Juarez was using as charges against me. There were no lengths to which he was not willing to go to incriminate me and bring about a sentence of death. There were three charges brought against me. First, the prosecutor presented letters, supposedly written by me at different times to Jose M. Gutierrez Estrada in Paris. According to these letters, I was supposed to be in favor of the Empire and the intervention of France in Mexico. Secondly, another letter, also published under my name, urging Archduke Maximilian to accept the call to the government that the Mexicans had given him. And, lastly, I was supposed to have commissioned Gutierrez Estrada in 1852 to offer the crown of the Mexican Empire to the courts of Europe.

These accusations were frauds, and when I was questioned about them, I answered angrily, "I have never seen these letters before. I did not write them, and to say that I did is to slander me. I have never had the honor of knowing the Archduke Maximilian, and I certainly have never been on such friendly terms with him as to be able to write to him in this manner. It is a well-known fact that he was not even courteous enough to invite me to return to my country. This surely would not have taken place if I had invited him to take over the country."

When I was questioned about hiring Gutierrez Estrada—such an exaggerated accusation—I replied, "This event does not even deserve to be mentioned. It is absurd and belongs to the past. However, as I am obliged to answer every question, I shall tell all that I know of the affair.

"My Minister of Foreign Affairs, Manuel D. Bonilla, gave the necessary orders to Estrada. No doubt,

Bonilla was prompted by his own ambition or that of his fellow party members. However, he exceeded his authority, and I only gained knowledge of the orders through a letter from Gutierrez Estrada. Estrada thanked me for the confidence I had placed in him and for the honor of the commission.

"I demanded that Minister Bonilla tell me why he had authorized such acts, and he told me, 'It is true that I wrote to Gutierrez. Before I took up the matter with the other Ministers, I wanted to see how the European courts received the idea.' Although I held Bonilla in high esteem, I ordered him to resign from the Cabinet. He did so the following day, asking me to forgive him for the trouble which his inadvertent actions had caused me.

"Now, everyone knows that Bonilla's reputation is an exalted one and that he belongs to a large and influential political party. His party members became angry over his dismissal, and I grew apprehensive. In order to avoid bad feelings, I had to accede to the petitions of his party and reinstate Bonilla. In order to do so, I had to keep silent about the cause of his removal from office. At the same time, I notified Gutierrez Esterada, officially and privately, to consider his transaction with Bonilla as null and void. No one gave the matter any more thought. To suggest that these actions, after so many years, have any bearing on recent events in this country is the height of ridiculousness."

The court then asked me what I had intended to

do in Vera Cruz in February of 1865, when the town was occupied by the French. They asked me whether I had recognized the intervention of France and the Empire, and if the name on the proclamation, issued at Orizaba, was mine. I knew that these questions were designed to trap me, and, adhering strictly to the truth, I answered, "My trip to Vera Cruz had no other purpose than to find out what was happening in the country. After all, I could not be indifferent to the affairs of my homeland. However, I failed in my quest. The French general, Bazaine, expelled me from the country immediately. This, in itself, should prove that I was not one of the advocates of French authority. I informed the government in power in Vera Cruz at that time of my arrival in their territory, just as duty demanded. On learning of the publication of the proclamation in Orizaba, I set out to contradict it through the press. However, before I could finish, the French had me expelled from the country. Surely, the most stupid critic could tell that the proclamation was not mine!"

This so-called "trial" then ended, and the case was turned over to the Council of Captains for the final sentence. There was an attempt to carry this farce even further by carrying me to Vera Cruz and exhibiting me before the people. However, I learned of the plot and stated resolutely, "Before another outrage like that one perpetrated at Campeche against me—before being jeered at and marched through streets sprinkled with my blood—I shall throw myself

213

into the sea." My defense attorney, Joaquin M. Alcalde, interprosed for me and the scandal was evaded.

The Council of Captains was composed of Juarez's henchmen. Juarez immediately raised the prosecuting attorney to the rank of Colonel, and, in order to show his gratitude, the prosecutor immediately demanded the death sentence. But, at this difficult time, my defense attorney proved his skill and courage. Disregarding the power and influence of Juarez, he painted a picture of my adherence to justice in bold relief. And he did not fail to touch on the iniquity of my enemies. His admirable eloquence so moved the voters, who were both poorly advised and inclined to evil, that they did not dare pronounce the death sentence.

Only to escape Juarez's wrath did they impose upon me an eight-year exile.[1] This sentence surprised many who were hoping for another.[2] Juarez, without hiding his spite, condemned the members of the Council of Captains to imprisonment in the fortress of Ulua for six months.

As no further reason was found to keep me in that wretched prison where I had been so tormented, I was put on an English packet boat bound for Havana, on November 1, 1867.

Queretaro

215

Santa Anna as Dictator of Mexico

216

Manual G. Pedraza

Tampico

218

Political cartoon depicting Santa Anna using the taxes of the Mexican nation for his own purposes

Mexico City in the mid-1800's

Military commission issued by Santa Anna as President of Mexico

General Juan Alvarez

Martin Carrera

Benito Juarez

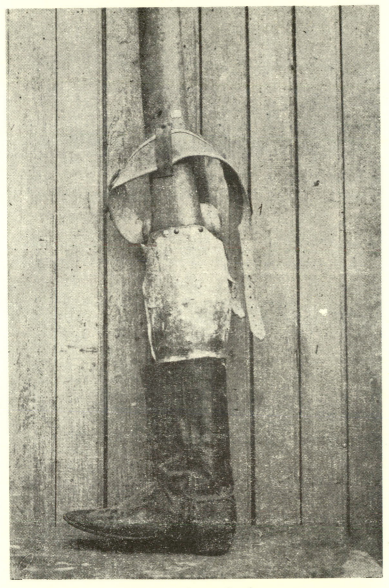

Santa Anna's wooden leg

225

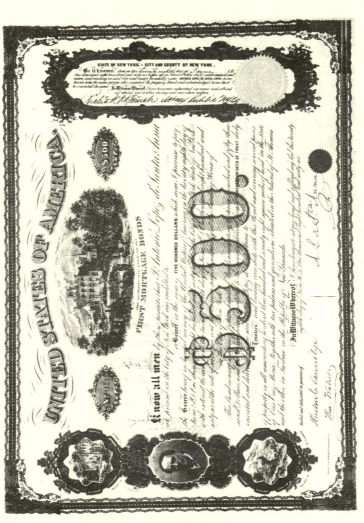

One of a number of mortgage bonds issued in New York City by Santa Anna to gain money for his campaign against the French intervention in Mexico. Santa Anna mortgaged his properties in Turbaco, Vera Cruz, and St. Thomas.

Santa Anna

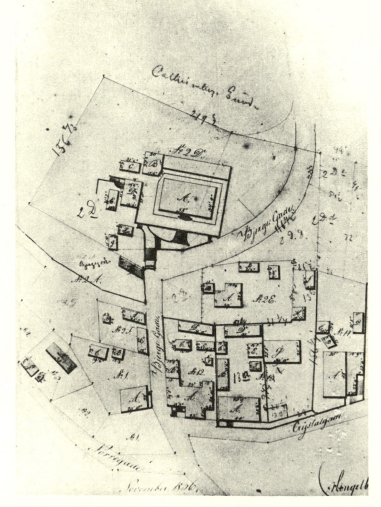

Charlotte Amalie, 1856 (Island of St. Thomas). The house and out buildings at the top were owned by Santa Anna.

First page of the manuscript of Santa Anna's autobiography.
Courtesy Latin-American Collection, University of Texas.

One of the last known photographs of Santa Anna, taken while he was working on his *Memoirs*

CHAPTER SEVENTEEN

The Plottings of Juarez—
My Last Journey to Nassau (1867-1872)

WHILE I was in prison in Havana, the agents of the suspicious and distrustful Juarez were busy plotting against me. Juarez used his advantageous position in my country's government to do me further harm. Not even the distance that separated us could keep this evil man from threatening me.

I had entrusted all my hopes to Secretary of State Seward, and my hopes had been destroyed. On looking back over the matter, I could not help but remember Seward's visit to San Tomas, his many conversations with me, and my visit to New York in search of aid for my country.

All my actions had been prompted by my love for my native country. My highest hopes and brightest dreams had been based on an opportunity to lead an expedition that would drive the French forever from Mexican territory. I had hoped for Seward's help in equipping an expedition, and I had hoped that Juarez would grant me an authorization to enter my country once more. As I have pointed out, Juarez insulted me gravely, and Secretary Seward had refused to receive my commission.

While I was locked in a dungeon in Ulua, a prisoner of the infamous Juarez, Seward revealed completely his total lack of concern toward me. In an official document he stated that my fate did not concern him in the least—callous and merciless words, considering that my fate was entirely at the mercy of the bloody Juarez. Seward's callousness could only please Juarez, especially after the negotiation of my bonds in New York.

My many misfortunes detained me in Havana, and Seward had another opportunity to ingratiate himself with Juarez, who had asked Seward to use his influence in having me expelled from Havana. Seward informed his consul to see that General Lirzundi carried out Juarez's orders. How can you explain such conduct on the part of a man who had disturbed my tranquillity in San Tomas and implored me to journey to New York! Such a trip and such unpleasant memories! I shall deplore this journey so long as I might live! I shall never forget the injuries I have suffered and the disillusions I have gained.

I was obliged, under the orders of the despotic Lirzundi, to leave Havana on a steamer destined for the islands of Santo Domingo, Puerto Rico, and San Tomas. I made up my mind to land at the first port we might touch, and I disembarked at Puerto de Plata and lived there for four months.

I had searched for peace and tranquillity, and I

found it in the city of Nassau. The generous hospitality of the people kept me there for four years. And I would have liked to have spent my last days there among those friendly natives, if obligations to my family did not call me to my native country.

I was still vigorous in constitution, and my fortunes changed for the better. The present was mine, and I pursued the future with eagerness. All my thoughts were for my country, which remained forever fixed in my mind. I was enthusiastic for the future of my country, and I resolved once more to encounter danger, conquer difficulties, and work incessantly for her welfare and glory. If my efforts are not sufficient to complete the work begun, it is because mortals are merely allowed to fill in the outlines. Perfection belongs to God. My footsteps merely point out the direction toward the coveted goal.

The account which I have written of my military and political history reveals the fact that vanity and glory have never moved me to take pen in hand. I have certainly never been guilty of such childish emotions! I have merely attempted to defend my honor—an honor so often maliciously attacked by the slander of the jealous.

When I close my eyes forever, I wish to be judged merely as I am, not as my enemies would have me be. If I were to ask for a title, it would merely be that of "Patriot." I leave to the understanding and conscientious reader to examine all the facts and draw his own conclusions as to my trustworthiness.

233

For my part, there are some deeds that are best covered with the veil of unstained patriotism for the sake of the honor of Mexico.

I have written these pages of history with a bold pen—with no other aid than my taxed memory. Unfortunately, much of the data which could have helped me prepare a more scrupulous account were burned at Manga de Clavo by United States soldiers in 1847. This infamous deed was performed in revenge for my having opposed the invasion. Other memoranda were robbed from me, along with my belongings, when I was in New-York. Therefore, I shall end this history, which I have written here in my tranquil home.

Several days ago I received news from my friends in Mexico that my evil enemy Juarez had listed my name among those he named as unfaithful to Mexico —people who had supported the Empire. Being informed of Juarez's plans, I was forced to reply. I immediately wrote the following protest, which I had printed and circulated.

PROTEST

"Antonio Lopez de Santa Anna: General of Division; *Benemerito de la Patria;* Ex-President of the Mexican Republic; Grand Master of the National and Distinguished Order of Guadalupe; Gran Cruz of the Order of Charles III of Spain, and similar rank in the Red Eagle of Prussia, decorated with honorary insignias and crosses for action in war.

"On the sad, but tranquil, island of New Providence, I have been waiting with a clear conscience and a firm will the establishment of order and justice in my unhappy country. I have been driven to this island by the partisan oppressor who has my unfortunate country in his power, and I have received the surprising news that the Mexican President has published a general amnesty for political crimes. In this amnesty he includes my name among those accused of being unfaithful to their country.

"What right has this tyrant to include me in this list? When have I ever been a traitor to my beloved country? When have I ever offended her? Who can accuse me? On what is this accusation based? Why does this treacherous man accuse me of treason? Disloyal to my country? The very word offends me. Only scum among the people would dare to believe and support this accusation.

"Struggling against foreign invaders, I lost my leg in the service of my country. I have sprinkled my country's soil with my sweat and blood. I have helped to establish equitable laws and have used my army to keep her safe from invasion. I am truly worthy of having played an important role in the history of the

235

most cultured nation of the civilized world.

"The name of Santa Anna has always been in the forefront of those who defended our country in times of danger. My voice joined with the boom of the cannons. I encountered death many times in the defense of my country's freedom. My country has been my master, and her soldiers, my brothers.

"How can that tyrant, so lacking in background, call me disloyal! Disloyal! I, the first leader of the Republic, sacrificed my dignity and self-esteem to write to him from New York, when he was a fugitive on the northern frontier, and to offer him my sword to help to shake off the yoke of the French.

"I should have known that my services would be greeted with coldness. This Indian tyrant is calling me disloyal in order to be able to sell my valuable property at a ridiculous price. He wishes to leave me without either bread or shelter. He has already deprived me of the salaries owed me for the many sacrifices I made to my country in the last span of my life. But, no matter how often this Indian may call me disloyal, I know all honorable men of my country will continue to honor me.

"This stroke of characteristic hypocrisy on the part of Benito Juarez forces me to protest energetically against the amnesty by which he hopes to humiliate me. Yes, I must protest of that Juarez, symbol of cruelty, whose services and deeds are written in blood on the ruins of our sacred temples and in the barbaric and grim sacrifices of our soldiers.

"Yes, I wish to protest of that Juarez, who, under the pretext of fighting for liberty, has constantly gnawed like so many worms at our fragile and vacillating social structure and has blasted the firm foundation of our religious beliefs.

"Yes, I wish to protest of that Juarez, whose right hand has never brandished the sword of a gentleman and soldier in defense of his country. But, indeed, this same hand has held the pen of the vulture—a pen used for decreeing banishments, for claiming property, and for decreeing assassinations.

"Yes, I wish to protest of that Juarez who made me suffer a horrible imprisonment in the dungeon of the castle of Ulua. The same Juarez who ordered his subordinate, the governor of Sisal, to trample upon the rights of both nations and persons by taking me from a foreign passenger ship. If the tyrant did not order my assissination, it was not through lack of will or through remorse for his evil deeds. He merely ordered that I be tried as a traitor. From this infamous snare, I escaped honorably, in spite of his malice. He merely failed to have me assassinated because of his own cowardice

—the cowardice of every tyrant, who spies the sword of justice across his crimes.

"Finally, I wish to protest of that Juarez, who, like a boa constrictor which surrounds and squeezes its victim to death, holds tortured Mexico in a death grasp.

"And this is the man who dares to include cynically the name of a grandee of Mexico in an amnesty of the unfaithful. He dares to include the name of the man who so gloriously gained independence on the banks of the Panuco. The man who drove the French back to their ships in Vera Cruz. The man who lost his leg in that memorable expedition. The man who improvised armies and fought so valiently on the fields of La Angostura, Cerro Gordo, and the Valley of Mexico.

"Treason! What sarcasm! Down with that miserable creature! I despise the pardon he has granted me! I prefer to die a thousand deaths than to bow my gray head to the executioner of my country.

"It is not the noble and humanitarian conduct of the worthy citizens of my nation that I am protesting in this document. No, as I believe in God, my heart swells with contentment when I see that there are in my country men of lofty sentiments who have known how to tame this savage. Men who have forced him to sign, with his bloody and sacreligious hand,

238

a law which he would have joyfully ripped apart. It is far, very far, from my noble sentiments to reproach the conciliatory work of the honorable Chamber of Deputies. These honorable men have recently opened the doors of our country to a considerable number of banished citizens that Juarez claimed were traitors. Good health to these noble representatives of the Mexican people! May they only receive this spontaneous outburst of mine as a pledge of my good faith and complete satisfaction for their deeds.

"My breast bursts with righteous indignation. I know it is time to break my silence. My recriminations are directed solely and exclusively against the wicked Juarez who, to our shame and to the disgrace of humanity, governs the destinies of my nation. This obscure Indian is attempting to blemish my patriotism and life-long service to my country.

"Where was this miserable tyrant when I fought for the independence of Mexico? Where was he when I stood on the banks of Vera Cruz, founding the very Republic which he boasts of guarding so zealously? Where was he when the French trampled our rights underfoot in Vera Cruz in 1838? Where was he when my blood mixed with the noblest Mexican blood?

"He lay like a hyena in his dirty retreat,

239

waiting only for the destruction of the leaders of the army. There he plotted his rise to power on the spoils of war. With loathing in my voice, I repeat, 'Down with the monster!'

> Antonio Lopez de Santa Anna
> Nassau, November 23, 1870"

Post Script

You will note from the date of the preceding *Memoirs* that I wrote them in a foreign country. I wrote them at a time when I was crushed with pain and emotion, and I spoke what was in my heart in these pages. Perhaps my language will appear to some to be rude at times. But, you must take into account the fact that undisguised truth is often severe. And the one who utters these truths should be granted a pardon. After all, I have been the victim of many torments, and I must expose the injustice of my cruel and inhuman enemies.

It is impossible for me not to be moved by the strongest feelings when I recall the evil deeds committed without reason or justice against me. My feelings can be nothing less than profound when I recall the evil vengeance that has so greatly injured my honor and interests. Such inhuman acts can, and must, arouse the indignation of even the most indifferent.

Perhaps, through ignorance, I might have committed acts deserving of censure during my long career of public service. But I can assure you that I

240

will give my word that my intentions have always been the most sincere, and I have directed my acts toward the glory and service of my country. Never have I deviated for even an instant from the path that duty and honor set before me. If my activities have been somewhat excessive, they have been prompted by my zeal and desire to serve my country to the fullest.

I believe that I have merited the title of a good patriot. Much as this fact will grieve my enemies, I am justly proud that my country has bestowed on me the title of *Benemerito de la Patria*. This honor will make me proud to the last day of my life. I have never desired riches, but to have earned the right to be known as a good citizen fulfills my every ambition.

One of the many slanders that has been heaped upon me is the tale of my great wealth. My exaggerated fortune has been claimed to amount into many millions of pesos. Since this malicious tale has been spread throughout the country, I merely wish to present the following in my self-defense.

The bond sent from New York and presented by Mr. John S. Darling on the first of the month was neither issued nor circulated in any form by me. Therefore, it had no status or value whatsoever. Why the bond has no value and how it came to be issued must be explained.

It was my deepest desire to aid my countrymen in driving the French from Mexican territory. The French domination was becoming more loathsome every day, and I had been offered aid for my country in the United States. I undertook a voyage to New York in May, 1866, but found I had been miserably deceived. I needed seven hundred fifty thousand pesos in gold in order to equip an expedition to Mexico.

Gabor Naphegyi, a native Hungarian, suggested the idea of a loan and offered to solicit creditors for the amount that I needed. Naphegyi introduced me to Henry G. Novton, head of the house of Novton, Virgil, Wilson and Company, and they agreed to make the loan. I was to present sufficient collateral as security for the amount I received and was to issue bonds with interest. The collateral and terms which I proposed were accepted and the contract was agreed upon. Naphegyi drew up the contract, and had both the contract and the bonds written out in English, which seemed wise to him. At the same time, he charged himself with legalizing them. He made all the arrangements with the greatest efficiency.

However, all our plans were useless. I found that my expedition to Mexico would be of no value. The governments of France and the United States signed a treaty, under the terms of which the French were to withdraw from Mexican territory at stated intervals. Of course, the contract which I had signed for the money was considered unnecessary and null and void. No one thought about the matter again, and the documents relating to the contract were discarded as useless.

In May, 1867, I left New York in a great hurry and could not attend to the discarded documents for some time. However, Naphegyi was put in charge of seeing that they were nullified. It was the furtherest thought from my mind that some people would take advantage of useless documents to serve their own avarice.

I was sailing on the steamer *Virginia* under the United States flag and bound for Havana, when I was assaulted and taken to shore by force. The *Virginia* was anchored outside Mexican waters, facing the port of Sisal. This violent and scandalous act was performed by the henchmen of that petty tyrant Juarez. I was completely within Juarez's power, and everyone thought that he would have me killed. Newspapers even announced my death.

Naphegyi took advantage of this sad occasion to further his business interests and to undermine me. The fallacious mortgage appeared in the records office of San Tomas, as my home was located there. A registered letter was also recorded. This letter from me to Naphegyi was supposedly to approve one of the very misdemeanors which I had actually reproved him for. I found out about these facts when I arrived in Havana.

I immediately took action, instructing Francisco Travesi to go to San Tomas and establish in the records office the nullified state of the mortgage and the falsity of the letter. Travesi complied with my instructions and presented the judge with a legal

243

protest in my name. This protest was registered in the records office and can be easily seen there.

Although Naphegyi's schemes failed to surprise me, those of Novton, who protected and stood by him, did. Novton even entered into a dispute with the Juarez government over the title to my hacienda, *El Encero,* which was also included in the mortgage. Such brazen effrontery can only be believed when it is seen! How could Novton have possibly acquired rights on my property, when he had never paid me one cent of the money! But some people will dare to do anything when they have no fear of reprisal.

What I have related is the absolute truth in relation to the matter of the bonds. In order that it may be recorded where and when it is fitting, I sign it here in Nassau, March 12, 1872.

Antonio Lopez de Santa Anna
Nassau, New Providence

Conclusion

H OW SHORT, indeed, is the life of man! How imperfect are his works, how insufficient his power, how insatiable his desire, how lively his hopes, and—alas, how sure his suffering!

Seventy-four years have flown by since that glorious day, when, as an adolescent, I first glimpsed, shining on my right arm, the silver epaulets of a cadet in the Royal Army of the land of my forefathers. How impatient I was to climb the stair of life! With the typical eagerness of youth, I wished to vault its steps two by two, four by four. But the course of every man is dictated by a wiser, more patient Nature.

Nevertheless, when I became a man, I looked back over the broad ocean of the past with an indefinable melancholy. Those same epaulets, which had glistened so brilliantly in my youth, seemed somewhat tarnished by the years. How swiftly these years had flown!

Every man who climbs the ladder of success is eulogized by those who lavish incense on the idol of power. Man is nothing; power, everything! When a man falls from his exalted and seemingly invulnerable position, the brutal, fickle throng heaps his head with curses and pursues him with sword and dagger drawn. The loftier the position of their idol, the more the hatred and persecution increase. Such deeds occur every day, and such deeds have I sadly experienced in my own life.

For eighteen years and six months I have endured a heartrending exile from my native land. My political enemies have pursued me relentlessly, heaping insults on my head. Nothing is sacred to them. They have drained me dry. They have wrenched from me all that I had gained during the many years of sacrifices by my sweat and blood. They have left me without a parcel of land, without a hut to shelter my bones, without a stone to lay my head on. And they have done this in complete secrecy. Why so much violence? Why so much cruelty?

Only my executioners can answer these questions. Violence and cruelty are the works of those men once in power. If it had not been for the help of my children, I would have died from want. I have drunk the cup of bitterness, drop by drop.

Nevertheless, I shall congratulate with the greatest of pleasure, the fortunate countryman who brings peace to our native land. It will be a glorious day when our children can say, "We have our own country, our own religion, our own law."

On this glorious day, I will forgive and forget the

grave offenses which I have suffered. On this day, I shall absolve the guilty for my many sufferings. There is no room in my heart for hatred or vengeance.

What is there left for me to say in these *Memoirs*? I can only make evident the injustice and ingratitude of my offenders. They have attacked my reputation both as a soldier and as head of my country. It only remains for me to make a short mention of my opportune and important services to my country—first, in fighting for and establishing independence in my country; then, in establishing the Republic; lastly, in being the first to shed blood in fighting my country's invaders.

But, before I lay down my pen, I wish to state the fact that I have always defended the Roman Catholic faith, the only one in which I believe and the one in which I must die. I was never neglectful of church property and allowed no one to confiscate it. My conscience and honor shall always be free from the taint of having enriched myself with the spoils of churches.

Religion! Ever the watchword of the Mexican people, when they proclaimed their emancipation from the Mother country! Their flag and standards bear the colors white, green, and red—symbolizing Religion, Independence, and Union. In less than a year, this magical theme had passed triumphantly through the land of the Anahuac. I cannot recall this happy time without emotion!

Oh, that my countrymen would only be convinced

that without the sanction of religious beliefs and the conservation of morality neither order or peace is possible. Law itself derives from Justice. But when Law is separated from Religion, it moves contrary to the purpose of Justice. Jean Jacques Rousseau once said: "Without the sanction of religion, I see only hypocrisy, injustice, and deceit in every man." Many people hold the opinion that social liberty should be the result of an organization based on the laws of moral order. Lazarga has said: "Liberty without moderation is conducive to anarchy."

The history of the Mexican Republic is not yet generally well known in its entirety. Our history has been corrupted by foreigners, who have undertaken to write an account of our life only from what is told to them. They do not know our vast land, populated by two distinct races, each with its different language, disposition, and customs. We are a land which has been admirably favored by Nature. Our country includes some states larger than many of the kingdoms of Europe.

The future will provide us with Mexican historians who will clear up many deeds and place truth in its correct light. Truth has the privilege of assuring the duration of all works which mark historic events, transmitting them to posterity.

Being constantly reproached by treacherous slanders from my insatiable enemies, I resolved to write and publish the true history of my public life. These *Memoirs* are a complete reply to their slanders

—sufficient in all ways to confront my enemies' absurd and ignoble lies with my own deeds. All who are burdened with the reading of my *Memoirs*, must surely see in my deeds only a patriot serving his nation to the best of his ability. I am confident that I will be worthy of my country's gratitude, and I have even greater confidence that posterity will do me full justice.

The End of The Story

Santa Anna's last years were lonely and unhappy ones. When he completed his *Memoirs* in 1874, he was eighty years old. Crippled and with cataracts almost blinding his eyes, he received the long-awaited news that Juarez had died and that the Liberal party had granted him political amnesty.

Once again the old general packed his meager belongings for the long trip back to Mexico. He and his wife landed at Veracruz and made the tedious trip to Mexico City by train. Members of his family and a handful of devoted old friends greeted them. How different from the days when thousands of cheering spectators eagerly greeted the Hero of Tampico!

Only a few newspapers took notice of the former hero. The *Monitor Republicano* of March 4, 1874, stated: "Mexico does not remember the great political errors of the man who so long controlled its destinies. . . . The Republic today stands with majesty on the throne of peace, and can forget mistakes and open its doors to the one it kept in exile so long."

Slighted by the government of Lerdo de Tejada, Santa Anna spent his days recalling the past with old friends. He visited the Shrine of Guadalupe, to which he had always paid homage. His friends took mercy on the penniless old man and started a movement to return his estates to him. Once again, the nation, spurred on by the newspapers, took sides against the old warrior. Finally, Congress granted pensions to all the soldiers who had helped win Mexico's independence. Santa Anna also secured some money from the estate of Manuel Escandon.

However, more direct blows to his pride were in the offing. Santa Anna was completely ignored by the President and the Cabinet when they celebrated the anniversary of the Battle of Churubusco. The general who had led the Mexican troops into battle on that occasion was left out of the ceremonies. In characteristic style, Santa Anna wrote a letter lauding his own feats at Churubusco, and the letter was published on the front page of the newspapers.

Gradually His Most Serene Highness slipped into senility. Aged, lame, and bitter, he died on June 21, 1876. Only a very few carriages followed him to his grave.

The newspapers took the nation to task for ignoring the passing of the once powerful dictator. *El Siglo Diez y Nueve* printed: "GENERAL SANTA ANNA— The last hours of his life inspire the saddest of reflections: the man who controlled millions, who acquired fortune and honors, who exercised an unrestricted dic-

251

tatorship, has died in the midst of the greatest want, abandoned by all except a few of his friends who remembered him in adversity. A relic of another epoch, our generation remembered him for the misfortunes he brought upon the republic, forgetting the really eminent services he rendered to the nation. He was as a tree, stricken in years, destitute of foliage, to whose boughs even such parasites as are usually found on dry and withered trees did not cling."

The *Two Republics* printed the following simple obituary:

"General Antonio Lopez de Santa Anna died in this city on the 21st inst.

"However he may have been condemned by parties, his career formed a brilliant and important portion of the History of Mexico, and future historians will differ in their judgment of his merits.

"General Santa Anna outlived his usefulness and ambition, and died at the ripe age of eighty-four. Peace to his ashes."

And with the passing of Santa Anna, passed an era of Mexico's history. Like the soaring flight of an eagle, Santa Anna's career had risen to the pinnacle and dipped to the bottom—but never into oblivion. He wrote one of the most colorful and fascinating pages in the history of Mexico. He called himself "The Napoleon of the West," and his career strangely parallels that of the little Corsican. Revered by some, hated by many, he remains "The Eagle," who once held all of Mexico in his grasp.

252

Notes

Notes

CHAPTER ONE

My Military and Political History—Beginnings

[1] Antonio Lopez de Santa Anna Perez de Lebron was born at Jalapa, Vera Cruz, on February 21, 1794, of middle-class Spanish parents. After limited schooling, ending in his fourteenth year, his father apprenticed him to a merchant. The young Santa Anna, however, aspired to a military career and was accepted as a cadet in the Fijo de Vera Cruz infantry regiment. Wilfrid Hardy Callcott, *Santa Anna*, 1–7.

[2] General Joaquin de Arredondo (1768–c. 1825) was virtual ruler of the North Mexican provinces from 1810 until Mexican Independence was achieved in 1821. His title was Commandant of the Eastern Division of the Provincias Internas, which comprised everything north of Monterey. He defeated Jose Alvarez de Toledo's revolt in the noted Battle of Medina River. He also scored victories over Hidalgo and Gauchupin revolts in 1812 and 1813, and over Xavier Mina's expedition of 1816–1817. He remained a Loyalist and retired to Cuba after Iturbide took power. Santa Anna, undoubtedly, saw a good deal of action while serving under Arredondo. Vita Alessio Robles, *Coahuila y Texas*, I.

[3] During these campaigns with Arredondo, Santa Anna lost heavily at the gambling tables. He forged the signatures of Colonel Quintero and General Arredondo on drafts on the company's funds. He said that he was trying to defend a brother officer and the honor of his regiment. The surgeon of his regiment, Jaime Garza, advanced him the sum to pay his debt, but confiscated his sword and his personal property. This forgery was to haunt him many times in later years. Callcott, *op. cit.*, 11–12.

[4] Augustin de Iturbide had formerly been a commander of the Royalist forces, but had been forced to retire on account of serious charges of embezzling funds. When he turned patriot and declared for the independence of Mexico under a limited monarchy, he was joined by Guerrero, Guadalupe Victoria, and Nicolas Bravo. Clarence R. Wharton, *El Presidente*, 3–5.

[5] Actually the assault on Vera Cruz had been unsuccessful. Santa Anna bribed an obliging citizen of Vera Cruz to open one of the city's gates, and he led his army into the Plaza. During the battle in a heavy downpour, many of his troops fled, abandoning their arms. However, Iturbide supplied him with reinforcements and he successfully took command of Vera Cruz. Frank C. Hanighen, *Santa Anna: The Napoleon of the West*, 19–20.

[6] The Vera Cruz populace objected to surrendering to Santa Anna, and Iturbide appointed Colonel Rincon to negotiate the surrender. After the

surrender, Rincon withdrew and Santa Anna became Commandant General. C. W. Raines, "Life of Antonio Lopez de Santa Anna," *Texas Magazine*, I, 86–90.

CHAPTER TWO

The Empire (1822–1823)—The Republic (1824–1825)

[1] The old revolutionary leaders Guadalupe Victoria, Guerrero, and Bravo headed the Republican party. They advocated putting aside the *Plan de Iguala* and establishing a Federal Republic. Arthur H. Noll, *From Empire to Republic*, 84.

[2] Santa Anna made overtures to the Spanish General Lemaur, commander of the Spanish troops at San Juan de Ulua. They agreed that the Spaniards might take possession of the city without meeting any resistance on the night of October 26, 1822. Santa Anna merely pretended to surrender and planned to capture the troops. The plan went awry, although the Spaniards were defeated. Hubert Howe Bancroft, *History of Mexico*, IV, 786–88.

[3] Jose Antonio Echavarri, Captain General of the provinces of Puebla, Vera Cruz, and Oaxaca, agreed to Santa Anna's schemes for the taking of San Juan de Ulua. However, Echavarri barely escaped death, as Santa Anna's force failed to arrive in time. Echavarri wrote to Iturbide that Santa Anna had purposely tried to cause his death or capture, as he was jealous that Echavarri had been appointed captain general. *Ibid.*, 787–88.

[4] Iturbide left Mexico City on November 10, 1822, supposedly to look over the situation at San Juan de Ulua. However, his prime purpose, owing to Echavarri's letter, was to remove Santa Anna as commandant of Vera Cruz. *Ibid.*, 788.

[5] When Iturbide had promoted Santa Anna from colonel to brigadier, Santa Anna had written to him, "Hail to Your Majesty for our glory, and let this expression be so gratifying that the sweet name of Augustin I will be transmitted to our descendants, giving them an idea of the memorable actions of our worthy Liberator. They will immortalize for history how just you are, and I together with my regiment, No. 8, was ready to give such a most worthy and glorious exaltation political support; we feel that we have not merely been the motivators of such a step but the first in this province who offered tribute to Your Majesty; yes, the first who offered our lives and persons to conserve the respectable existence of Your Majesty and the crown which you so worthily obtained, remaining as we are constant subordinates who will shed our blood for the most worthy

Emperor." Quoted in Hanighen, *op. cit.*, 23.

[6] Apparently Iturbide greeted Santa Anna warmly and tried to soften the blow of his removal. He offered Santa Anna a post in the capital, saying, "I await you in Mexico, Santa Anna, to make your fortune for you." Santa Anna said later that he knew he was going to be removed, and only asked to be allowed to set his affairs in order. As he was sitting at the table with Iturbide, an aide-de-camp entered and sternly reproached Santa Anna: "In the Emperor's presence one should always stand at attention." *Ibid.*, 26.

[7] Jose Antonio Echavarri, a native Spaniard, adhered to the cause of the Revolution in 1821. He was a great favorite of Iturbide, but he was greatly influenced by members of the Masonic Order and defected from Iturbide's Empire. Bancroft, *op. cit.*, IV, 793–96.

[8] Santa Anna had been joined by the old revolutionary Guadalupe Victoria. Santa Anna stormed Jalapa on December 21, 1822, suffering a devastating defeat. Santa Anna fled to join Victoria at Puente del Rey, where he suggested that they both flee to the United States. But Victoria told him: "Go and put Vera Cruz in a state of defence. You can set sail when they show you my head." *Ibid.*, 792.

[9] The *Plan de Casa Mata* guaranteed a republican form of government to Mexico. Also, the army agreed to reconvene the national representative Congress. *Ibid.*, 795.

[10] Iturbide actually established Mexican independence, but set up a form of despotism as absolute as that of Spain. Santa Anna started the movement that resulted in the Republic. However, Santa Anna was lacking in character and principles. General O'Donoju, who knew him well, said of him, "This young man will live to make his country weep." Wharton, *op. cit.*, 19.

[11] The Constitution of 1824 provided for a republican form of government. Although it incorporated many features of the Constitution of the United States, the people were never made aware of their duties or their responsibilities.

[12] Victoria swore to protect the Constitution and tried to do so throughout his days in office. He was honest and tried to govern with justice and mercy. However, his vice-president was Nicolas Bravo, who favored a centralized government and was supported by the conservatives, clericals, and Spaniards. Hanighen, *op. cit.*, 31–32.

[13] Santa Anna was sent to Yucatan to get him out of the capital. Before Guadalupe Victoria was elected president, Santa Anna entertained the idea of having himself made Emperor instead of Iturbide. According to

one biographer, he hired men to run through the streets, shouting, "Long live Anthony the First." Santa Anna was neither in the councils nor the confidence of either Victoria or Bravo. Wharton, *op. cit.*, 20–25.

[14] Santa Anna's government in Yucatan was one long series of disputes, but did manage to leave it in peace. At one time Santa Anna considered conquering Cuba and adding it to the Mexican Republic. When the Mexican foreign minister, Gomez Pedraza, heard of his bold plan, he said, "If it succeeds it ought to be a great honor for Mexico. If it fails, at least, it will rid us of Santa Anna." Hanighen, *op. cit.*, 34–35.

[15] Fearing that Iturbide would again gain power in Mexico, the Congress passed a decree on April 28, 1824, sentencing him to death should he ever enter Mexico again. Iturbide landed at Soto la Marina on July 14, 1824, unaware of the death decree. The Congress of Tamaulipas passed his death sentence, and Iturbide was shot at Padilla on July 19, 1824. Bancroft, *op. cit.*, IV, 804–10.

[16] Mango de Clavo was conveniently located on the road from Jalapa to Vera Cruz. Santa Anna purchased it for twenty-five thousand pesos, he said. He lived there with his wife, Inez Garcia, and their children. One legend maintains that Santa Anna desired Inez's prettier sister, but his proposal to the parents was so awkward that he was engaged to Inez. Only when he approached the altar did he note the mistake. However, Santa Anna shrugged and said, "It's all the same to me." Quoted in Hanighen, *op. cit.*, 38–39.

CHAPTER THREE

The Election of Vicente Guerrero (1828)—The Spanish Invasion (1829)

[1] Guerrero was the candidate of the Federalist party and Pedraza was the candidate of the Centralist party. The Centralist party was composed of adherents to the Scottish rite Masons (Escocesses). The Federalists were mostly adherents of the York rite Masons (Yorkinos). Joel R. Poinsett, minister to Mexico from the United States, was credited with beginning the organization of York rite Masons in Mexico. The Yorkinos stood for liberalism and republicanism. Santa Anna's brother edited a Scottish rite paper, and apparently Santa Anna became a member of the Scottish rite group. Lucas Alaman states that he actually saw proofs of Santa Anna's membership in the order when he was Governor of Yucatan. An unsupported story quoted by both previous biographies also suggests that Santa Anna escaped death at San Jacinto in 1836 by giving the Masonic distress signal to John A. Wharton, who had founded the first Masonic lodge in Texas. Callcott, *op. cit.*, 61–63. Also, Wharton, *op. cit.*, 22–28.

Notes

[2] Santa Anna's hatred of Pedraza stemmed from Pedraza's order to have him court martialed while in Yucatan. Generals Rincon and Calderon pursued Santa Anna and forced him to flee to Oaxaca. Revolution was declared in the capital, and Rincon and Calderon marched back, leaving Santa Anna free to resume his position as Governor of Vera Cruz. Hanighen, *op. cit.*, 43–50.

[3] Somewhat hesitantly Congress elected Guerrero president and Bustamante vice president. Bustamante was a conservative, and opposed many of Guerrero's plans. Guerrero's elevation to the Presidency was a triumph of the popular party. He believed in leaving the people to themselves and in maintaining federal institutions. Unfortunately, Mexico was not ready for such a liberal government, and the social and political ties were loosened. Hubert Howe Bancroft, *op. cit.*, V, 75–77.

[4] Santa Anna was severely criticized for setting off on this reckless adventure without any orders. He left the chief seaport of the country practically unguarded against the Spanish fleet. Callcott, *op. cit.*, 72.

[5] When Santa Anna began this campaign, an old veteran of the Napoleonic wars had said to him, "This campaign may do for you what Napoleon's Egyptian campaign accomplished for him." Shortly afterwards, Santa Anna began to refer to himself as "The Napoleon of the West." Quoted in Hanighen, *op. cit.*, 53.

[6] General Mier y Teran actually led most of the fighting in the battles. The promotion was awarded Santa Anna before the surrender of the Spaniards and could not have been a reward for it. Hanighen, *op. cit.*, 54–57. Also, Callcott, *op. cit.*, 77.

[7] The city of Tampico had its name officially changed to Santa Anna de Tamaulipas. When he reached Vera Cruz, he was greeted with parades and banquets. Jalapa and Vera Cruz vied with each other in doing him honor. Callcott, *op. cit.*, 77.

[8] Bustamante claimed a need for a more conservative government, but actually he, and his confederates, could not stand the fact that an Indian was head of the government. They destroyed a government whose only faults were excessive liberalism and clemency. Santa Anna tried to prevent the movement, and not succeeding, surrendered both his civil and military commands. Bancroft, *op. cit.*, V, 88–89.

[9] Guerrero's death was considered a murder and three ministers, Facio, Alaman, and Espinosa were impeached for having planned it. However, they were never convicted. *Ibid.*, 100.

259

Notes

CHAPTER FOUR
The Vera Cruz Act—Pedraza Becomes President (1832)

[1] Santa Anna was convinced that only a resort to arms could remove the dangers of a wide-spread revolution that would lead to anarchy. Bancroft, *op. cit.*, V, 107.

[2] Peaceful means were first tried. Alaman and Facio tried to convince Santa Anna to abandon the idea of a revolution. Facio even tried to bribe Jose Maria Flores, the commandant of San Juan de Ulua, to surrender Vera Cruz. However, Flores remained loyal and refused. *Ibid.*, 109.

[3] A reform movement had been started under General Mier y Teran, but the General became depressed over the state of the country and committed suicide. Gomez Farias, leader of the revolt against Bustamente in Zacatecas, obtained Santa Anna's consent to allow Gomez Pedraza's return to the Presidency. Hanighen, *op. cit.*, 66–68.

[4] Santa Anna knew that soon his time would come, and he acted the part of the modest, retiring patriot. He cried, "My entire ambition is to exchange the sword for the plow. If any hand again disturbs the public peace, Mexicans, do not forget me; I shall return to your call and we will make the world see that tyrants and oppressors cannot stay in the Mexican Republic." *Ibid.*, 69.

CHAPTER FIVE
My Election as President—The Texas Campaign (1833–1836)

[1] Bancroft states that Gomez Farias took possession of the government on the first of April, 1833, and appointed his Cabinet. Santa Anna decided that if he took over the Presidency, he could further the causes of the privileged classes, the military, and the church. Santa Anna assumed the presidential authority on the 16th of May, 1833. Bancroft, *op. cit.*, V, 131–32.

[2] Santa Anna was apparently made captive by his own troops. But his captors, to win the favor of the army, proclaimed him dictator, the very title he secretly wished for, *Ibid.*, 132–33.

[3] Santa Anna had the support of the army, but desired the backing of the clergy. He failed to support any one program for change. Callcott, *op. cit.*, 113.

[4] The *Plan de Cuernavaca*, issued May 23, 1835, appointed Santa Anna as the only existing upholder of the Constitution. This *Plan* gave Santa Anna the right to dissolve Congress. The object of the *Plan* was to proclaim religion, rights, and Santa Anna and to denounce reform, federation, and Gomez Farias. Bancroft, *op. cit.*, V, 140.

Notes

[5] Mexico gained its independence from Spain in 1821. She gained much of the land north of the Rio Grande from Spain at that time. In December, 1820, Moses Austin, then living in Missouri, applied to the Spanish authorities to bring three hundred American families to Texas to form a colony. Permission was granted, and when Stephen F. Austin presented his petition to Iturbide, it was ratified. During the years 1823–1832, Mexico encouraged emigration to the colony, and in 1832, there were probably 20,000 people residing in Texas. Under the Constitution of 1824, the Texans hoped for a republican form of government. When Santa Anna declared the Constitution of 1824 invalid, Stephen F. Austin led a group of Texans to Mexico to negotiate for adequate arrangements and was thrown into jail. Hanighen, *op. cit.*, 79–80. Also, Wharton, *op. cit.*, 46–47. Bancroft, *op. cit.*, V, 151–64.

[6] In view of Mexico's hostile attitude toward the colonists, the Texans decided to sever all connections with Mexico. They met in convention at Washington-on-the-Brazos on March 2, 1836, and adopted a declaration of independence. Bancroft, *op. cit.*, V, 166.

[7] Many of Santa Anna's old enemies lent moral support to the Texans. Gomez Farias solicited aid in New Orleans, and Lorenzo de Zavala, a firm believer in Federalist principles and Santa Anna's dreaded enemy, was named vice president of the Republic of Texas under Burnet. Callcott, *op. cit.*, V, 122–23. Also, Hanighen, *op. cit.*, 80–81.

[8] General Martin Perfecto de Cos was Santa Anna's brother-in-law. He had been sent to Texas to investigate the refusal of the Texans (including William Barret Travis) at Anahuac, to pay duties or imports to Mexico. Cos imprudently dismissed the Legislature of Coahuila and Texas, landed five hundred men at Matagorda, and established headquarters at San Antonio. He announced his intention of driving out all the American settlers in Texas, with the exception of those who had been in the region for longer than five years. General Edward Burleson and Colonel Ben Milam, with a force of volunteer militia, resisted, besieged San Antonio, and routed Cos' army. After an unconditional surrender in December, 1835, Cos and his men were released. Cos signed a written pledge that he would never return to Texas. Then he simply crossed the Rio Grande, rejoined Santa Anna's army, and returned with him into Texas a few weeks later. H. Bailey Carroll and Walter Prescott Webb, eds., *The Handbook of Texas*, I, 419.

[9] The Texas army had remained in San Antonio after defeating Cos. William B. Travis commanded the army, after all but about 150 of the militia men returned home. Travis received some 35 replacements, mak-

ing a total of about 187 men. Amelia Williams, "Critical Study of the Siege of the Alamo," *Southwestern Historical Quarterly*, XXXVII, 5.

[10] William B. Travis' letter stated, "I am still here in fine spirits. With one hundred and forty men I have held this place against a force variously estimated at from fifteen hundred to six thousand; and I shall continue to hold it till I get relief from my countrymen, or I will perish in its defense." A later letter read, "I feel confident that the determined valor and desperate courage heretofore evinced by my men will not fail them in the last struggle; and although they may be sacrificed to the vengeance of a Gothic enemy, the victory will cost so dear, that it will be worse for him than a defeat. God and Texas! Victory or death!" Original in the Texas State Library, Austin, Texas.

[11] The "self-styled" used here is apparently a retort to Houston's caustic comment that Santa Anna was "the self-styled Napoleon of the West." Houston had been appointed Commander-in-Chief of the Texas army by the Convention of 1836, shortly after the signing of the Texas Declaration of Independence.

[12] This letter, if it ever existed, is now unknown. Houston had two small six-pound field pieces known as the "Twin Sisters," the total artillery of the Texas army after the fall of the Alamo. Winkler, "The 'Twin Sisters' Cannon, 1836–1865," *Southwestern Historical Quarterly*, XXI, 61–68.

[13] Santa Anna supposedly delayed his attack on the Alamo, waiting for reinforcements from General Tolsa. Legend has it that Santa Anna met an attractive young girl, who further delayed his campaign. Unable to convince her mother that she should give him the girl unlawfully, he arranged a bogus wedding ceremony with one of his soldiers dressed as a priest. When he left the town of San Antonio, Santa Anna banished the girl to San Louis Potosi, where she supposedly bore his child. Hanighen, *op. cit.*, 86–88. Also, Callcott, *op. cit.*, 131–33.

[14] General Cos is said to have brought Travis and Crockett to Santa Anna and implored him to spare their lives, saying, "Mr. President, you have here two prisoners. In the name of the Republic of Mexico, I supplicate you to guarantee the lives of both." Santa Anna, in a rage, answered, "General, my order was to kill every man in the Alamo," and turning to some privates near by said, "Soldiers, kill them." Quoted in Hanighen, *op. cit.*, 94.

[15] Santa Anna's original report stated, "The Alamo was taken, this victory that was so much and so justly celebrated at the time, costing us seventy dead and about three hundred wounded. . . ." Carlos E. Casta-

neda, "Antonio Lopez de Santa Anna, Manifesto Relative to His Operations in the Texas Campaign and His Capture," *The Mexican Side of the Texan Revolution*, 14.

[16] Although Santa Anna seems to have no trouble remembering his own exploits, the men against whom he fought seem not to stand out in his memory. Throughout the narrative, he refers to many of the leaders of Texas by erroneous names. As in this case, Santa Anna's spelling is retained, with corrections in brackets. Here Santa Anna refers to Colonel James W. Fannin.

[17] Fannin's men, from all other accounts, Mexican and Texan alike, numbered between 325 and 450. In the massacre following Fannin's surrender, 342 were killed and some 24 escaped. Jose Urrea, *Diario de las Operaciones Militaries . . . en la Campana de Tejas*. Also Davenport, "Men of Goliad," *Southwestern Historical Quarterly*, XLIII.

[18] There is much contradiction over Fannin's surrender. Although he surrendered unconditionally to Urrea, Urrea recommended mercy. Santa Anna says that Urrea had the prisoners shot before reporting to him, but Urrea's communication to Santa Anna is stated here:
"Ministry of War and Marine
    Central Section
      Desk No. 1
Surrender of the force at Goliad under the command of James W. Fannin
"Art. 1. The Mexican troops having placed their battery one hundred and sixty paces from us and the fire having been renewed, we raised a white flag; Colonel Juan Morales, Colonel Mariano Salas, and Lieutenant Colonel of Engineers Juan Jose Holzinger came immediately. We proposed to surrender at discretion and they agreed.

"Art. 2. The commandant Fannin and the wounded shall be treated with all possible consideration upon the surrender of all their arms.

"Art. 3. The whole detachment shall be treated as prisoners of war and shall be subject to the disposition of the supreme government.

"Camp on the Coleto between the Guadalupe and La Bahia, March 20, 1836—B. C. Wallace, Commandant.—I. M. Chadwick, Aide.—approved, James W. Fannin.

"Since, when the white flag was raised by the enemy, I made it known to their office that I could not grant any other terms than an unconditional surrender and they agreed to it through the officers expressed, those who subscribe the surrender have no right to any other terms. They have been informed of this fact and they are agreed. I ought not, cannot, nor wish to grant any other terms—Jose Urrea."

Santa Anna in his report says, "Because of the execution of Fannin and his men I am accused of being barbarous and sanguinary. . . . The prisoners of Goliad were condemned by law, by a universal law, that of personal defence, enjoyed by all nations and all individuals. They surrendered unconditionally, as the communication of General Urrea shows. How could I divert the sword of justice from their heads without making it fall upon my own? . . . I could not, therefore, pardon these unfortunates. It has been said that they were protected by a capitulation, and, although the communication of General Urrea denies such a statement, I have asked the supreme government that an investigation be instituted to prove that neither officially nor confidentially was I notified of such a capitulation. . . . " In a later report, Santa Anna says, "The commandant at Goliad, Lieutenant Colonel Jose Nicolas de la Portilla, is responsible for the cruel and inhumane manner of carrying out the execution to the nation, to the world, and to God." Castaneda, *op. cit.*, 18–63.

[19] Houston's men were leaving the army in large numbers. Some were deserting and some had obtained permission to assist their families in retreating before Santa Anna's onslaught.

[20] Among those escaping were President David G. Burnet and his Cabinet.

[21] This letter is also unknown, although Santa Anna's papers were captured with him at San Jacinto. If this letter existed, it would help to explain Houston's intentions during his retreat. Burnet had written to Houston about this time: "Sir: The enemy are laughing you to scorn. You must fight them. You must retreat no farther. The country expects you to fight. The salvation of the country depends on your doing so." Burnet's letter was written April 7, 1836, and was published in the *Telegraph and Texas Register* (Houston), June 9, 1841, when Houston and Burnet were opposing candidates for the Texas Presidency.

[22] Both Urrea and Filisola claimed the other was at fault. Filisola claims that his army was dispersed, lacking in supplies, and sick. "The greatest part of our armament was in sad need of repair, and we did not even have a gunsmith." Urrea claims that Filisola should not have retreated. "Representation Addressed to the Supreme Government by General Vicente Filisola" in Castaneda, *op. cit.*, 172–202.

[23] Cos' men numbered 540, raising Santa Anna's total strength to the neighborhood of 1,350, five hundred more than the strength of Houston's forces. Marquis James, *The Raven*, 249.

[24] This courier, captured by Erastus "Deaf" Smith on April 18, 1836, was using Travis' saddlebags. One look at "Deaf" Smith and his Texas

guerilla spy company was probably sufficient torture to get him to talk. *Ibid.*, 244.

[25] Legend has it that Santa Anna had a mulatto girl, Emily Morgan, in his tent. William Bollaert states, "The Battle of San Jacinto was probably lost to the Mexicans, owing to the influence of a Mulatto Girl (Emily) belonging to Colonel Morgan, who was closeted in the tent with General Santana [sic], at the time the cry was made 'the enemy! they come! they come!' and detained Santana so long that order could not be restored readily again." W. Eugene Hollon and Ruth Laphan Butler, eds., *William Bollaert's Texas*, 108n. Colonel James Morgan was supposed to have mentioned the incident in a letter to Samuel Swartout, collector of the port of New York, when Morgan sent Swartout the silken tent in which Santa Anna and Emily were staying. Several Mexican historians have mentioned the incident and Frank Tolbert attaches credulity to the legend. The Texas song "The Yellow Rose of Texas" was supposedly written about Emily.

[26] Santa Anna states that he had ordered General Castrillon to keep strict watch and inform him of the slightest move from the enemy. He then states that he has positive evidence that Castrillon was shaving and changing his clothes. While the enemy attacked, Castrillon was whiling away his time in a party with other officers of his staff. Antonio Lopez de Santa Anna, "Manifesto Relative to His Operations in the Texas Campaign and His Capture," Document 9 in Castaneda, *op. cit.*, 81.

[27] Santa Anna seems to want to leave the impression that he was captured at this time. This neither agrees with Houston's account of the capture nor with Santa Anna's own account in his "Manifesto." In this document, Santa Anna states that he fled on horseback and attempted to join Filisola's troops at Thompson's Crossing. Santa Anna changed into other clothes, and the soldiers who captured him did not recognize him. He says that he was "taken before Houston on the 22nd of April, the day I was captured." He was actually taken prisoner in civilian clothes by General Burleson's scout, James A. Sylvester. *Ibid.*, 78–83.

[28] Vicente Filisola, *Representacion Dirigida al Supremo Gobierno por el General Vicente Filisola, en Defensa de Su Honor y Aclaracion de Sus Operaciones como General en Gefe del Ejercito sobre Tejas* (Mexico City, 1836). This work initiated a flurry of other buck-passing defences by Mexican leaders of the campaign, including Urrea, Cos, and Santa Anna himself. Filisola in 1848 wrote an additional "defence," *Memorias para la Historia de la Guerra de Tejas,* and another in 1849 under a similar title. He stood trial for his actions in Mexico City after his return in

265

August of 1836, and was completely exonerated. Streeter, *Bibliography of Texas*, III, 144–45.

[29] Juan Nepomuceno Almonte, supposedly the bastard child of the revolutionary priest, Morelos, was educated in the United States and had visited Texas several times before the 1836 campaign. After returning to Mexico with Santa Anna in 1837, he embarked on a rather spotted career. He was Minister to Belgium, Minister to the United States, Secretary of War during the Mexican War, Minister to England, and Minister to France. He sold out to the French, returning to Mexico in 1862 with Maximilian. He served briefly as "Supreme Chief of the Nation," in order to bring Maximilian to the throne. He died in 1869. Helen W. Harris, The Public Life of Juan Nepomuceno Almonte (Unpublished Ph.D. Thesis. The University of Texas), 1935; also *Diccionario Encyclopedia Hispano-Americano*, 1887.

[30] Thomas Jefferson Rusk, Secretary of War, who later served as first United States Senator from Texas. When Houston left for New Orleans on May 5, 1836, he commissioned Rusk Brigadier General and placed him in charge of the army.

[31] Santa Anna was kept closely guarded after a scheme was discovered to help Santa Anna escape. Bancroft, *op. cit.*, V, 174-75.

[32] On leaving, Santa Anna wrote to his captors:

"My Friends, I consider you brave on the field of battle, and generous after it. You can always count on my friendship, and you may never regret the consideration you have shown me. On returning to the country of my birth, through your kindness, please accept this sincere Farewell, from your grateful

Ant. Lopez de Santa Anna

Velasco, June 1st 1836
Witnesses:
Ramon Martinez Caro
Juan N. Almonte
Bailey Hardeman
Lorenzo de Zavala"

"Autograph of the Quarter," *Manuscripts*, XIV, No. 3 (Summer, 1962), citing the collection of M. H. Loewenstern, Amarillo, Texas.

[33] Although there was an offer from Jackson, Santa Anna makes no mention of the Treaty of Velasco, signed a few months before, wherein Santa Anna agreed to recognize the independence of Texas, with the state's boundaries set at the Rio Grande. In line with this treaty, Santa

Anna asked Jackson for assistance, and it was Jackson who refused, on the basis that Santa Anna was not the official government of Mexico. These events are described in *Message from the President . . . Transmitting His Correspondence with General Santa Anna . . .* (Washington, January 18, 1837), 1–5.

CHAPTER SIX
My Resignation as President—The Defense of Vera Cruz (1837–1838)
[1] The so-called Pastry War of 1838 arose over claims of Frenchmen in Mexico against the Mexican government. A French subject, a baker, pressed a claim against the Mexican government when his shop with all its merchandise was destroyed in 1828, when the Parian was sacked. Bancroft, *op. cit.*, V, 186–191. Also, Wharton, *op. cit.*, 73–75.

[2] Commander David Farragut was aboard an American warship and watched the French bombardment of the fortress. He reported, "I visited the Castle to ascertain the cause of its early surrender and a single glance satisfied me that it would have been impracticable for the Mexicans to stand to their guns. The very material which formerly insured their safety was now a means of destruction, for the Castle is built of a sort of limestone resembling coral . . . a shell . . . would expload and rend the stone in immense masses, killing and wounding the men at the guns, in many instances shattering the walls from summit to foundation. I am perfectly satisfied that in a few hours more it would have been a mass of rubbish. Only picture to yourself a shower of two hundred shell and shot falling into a castle! Davis told me a man might stay there and be killed, but it was impossible to do anything, for he was not on his feet five minutes before he was knocked down again by a fragment of wood or stone." Quoted in Hanighen, *op. cit.*, 147–48.

[3] Gaona could do nothing but surrender the city, but Santa Anna would not agree. He spread the report that the surrender was made over his protest. Gaona was court martialed for having surrendered, and Santa Anna took over the command of the army. Wharton, *op. cit.*, 74.

[4] Santa Anna supposedly ran naked from the room, clutching his clothes about him. The French soldiers let the frightened little man pass, merely asking him, "Where is Santa Anna?" Santa Anna pointed to the room where Arista was sleeping and said, "There!" Raines, *op. cit.*, 124.

[5] Bancroft states that, "Santa Anna, meanwhile, had kept himself at a safe distance, collecting what troops he could and waiting for the summoned force of Arista. Learning of the retrograde march, however, he thought the moment had arrived to share in the credit earned by the de-

267

fenders of the barracks, by pretending to chase the French." Bancroft, *op. cit.*, V, 198.

⁶ Santa Anna's leg wound proved quite serious, and he was taken to Pozitos, where his leg was amputated. The job was poorly done, and Santa Anna suffered considerable pain for the rest of his days. The leg was carried with Santa Anna to Manga de Clavo, and later transferred to Mexico City and placed in a ceremonial resting place. Santa Anna wrote a florid report to the Minister of War, which was printed as a broadside and widely circulated in Mexico City. He stated, "*We conquered, yes, we conquered:* Mexican arms secured a glorious victory in the plaza; and the flag of Mexico remained triumphant: I was wounded in this last effort and probably this will be the last victory that I shall offer my native land.

"On closing my career, I cannot refrain from expressing my joy at seeing the beginnings of reconciliation among the Mexican factions. . . .

"I ask also of the government of my country that my body be buried in this same soil *(medanos)* so that my companions in arms may know that this is the line of battle I leave marked out for them: that from this day forward the most unjust of Mexican enemies shall not dare to place their feet on our soil. I demand of my fellow countrymen also that they do not stain our victory by attacking the indefensible Frenchmen, who live among us under the protection of our laws. . . .

"May all Mexicans, forgetting my political mistakes, not deny me the only title which I wish to leave my children: that of a 'good Mexican.'" Callcott, *op. cit.*, 159.

CHAPTER SEVEN

The Revolution—The Presidency Again—Exile (1841–1844)

¹ Bustamente, first constitutional president under the Constitution of 1836, was faced with the dilemma of leaving Santa Anna in the capital or of letting him go to the front in his place. He had difficulty in deciding, and Santa Anna said to him, "I did not come here to take your place from you: I have been brought without wishing it. I advise you as a friend to go to Tampico, because if you do not, the evil will grow greatly, and when you wish to do so you will not be able to control it. If you do not go I shall, in spite of my physical condition." Bustamente went, and the President of the Council, who should have taken Bustamente's place according to the Constitution, was sick. Therefore, Congress enthusiastically selected Santa Anna as president. Quoted in Callcott, *op. cit.*, 161.

² Bancroft states that, "Popular approval naturally followed the winning side, but any change was now welcomed as an improvement, and

268

the hero of Vera Cruz seemed the most promising man for the occasion. A spectator could not fail to be impressed by his tall, graceful figure, with its small oval face stamped by thought and energy, and with the closely set eyes, brilliantly reflecting an impulsive nature and a talented mind. A sprinkling of gray in the black hair added dignity, and the dark, bilious complexion, with its striking expression of anxious melancholy hovering round the mouth when in repose, generally brightened during conversation into sympathizing affability and winning smiles. When giving command the voice assumed a well balanced, dictatorial tone, which was effectively imposing, and when roused his face changed into repelling fierceness." Bancroft, *op. cit.*, V, 236–37.

[3] These *Bases*, issued on September 28, 1841, provided for the naming of deputies from the various departments by the Commander-in-Chief of the army. These deputies composed a junta, who had the power to name a provisional President. The President would in turn summon a Congress in order to frame a new Constitution. Santa Anna as Commander-in-Chief of the army selected the deputies, and they returned the compliment by naming him provisional President. *Ibid.*, V, 233–37.

[4] Santa Anna's many reforms were outweighed by his many despotic acts. *Ibid.*, V, 241.

[5] Santa Anna's first wife, Dona Ines Garcia, died in Puebla on August 23, 1844, at the age of thirty-three. Santa Anna mentions four children by her in his will: two boys, Antonio (who died as a child), and Manuel; as well as two daughters, Maria Guadalupe and Maria del Carmen. There was talk of another child who suffered from a mental affliction. Santa Anna was embarrassed to have the child seen in public, and Dona Ines devoted herself to his care. Although Santa Anna had been genuinely fond of Dona Ines, he wasted no time in taking another wife. He cut short the official mourning period to marry a fifteen-year-old girl, Senorita Maria Doloras Tosta. Callcott, *op. cit.*, 200–204.

[6] Paredes had sound support for his revolution from the many enemies of Santa Anna. Numerous indictments of Santa Anna's autocracy appeared in print. One read, "Genius of evil (Santa Anna) and covetousness! you are like Atilla the scourge of God! Your power has been like that of Satan, a power of corruption, of ruin and destruction! You resemble a fury of hell, blind, devestating and bloody! Amid the horrors of civil war, amid lakes of blood and mountains of dead bodies you always present yourself like a spectre, inciting all to devestation, slaughter, and revenge, etc." Quoted in Hanighen, *op. cit.*, 188.

[7] Canalizo, called the "Lion of the Guadalupe" because he had re-

mained faithful to Bustamente, had dissolved the Congress which had voted against Santa Anna. Rebellion followed, and Canalizo was imprisoned and the Congress reassembled. General Jose Joaquin de Herrera, President of the Council, rose to the Presidency. Noll, *op. cit.*, 152.

[8] Santa Anna tried to escape disguised as a muleteer. However, he was ambushed by a tribe of Indians and taken to their settlement. There the Indians forced him to go through a crude and torturous ceremony. They planned to boil him in a huge cauldron after wrapping him in banana leaves and spices. He was to be boiled until he was dead but the flesh still firm. Then wrapped as a giant tamale, he was to be turned over to the authorities. Santa Anna only escaped this bizarre fate through the intervention of the local priest. Quoted in Callcott, *op. cit.*, 212–13. Also, Bancroft, *op. cit.*, V, 277.

[9] Although Santa Anna protested his imprisonment, the grand jury of Congress called for his impeachment on the grounds that he had attacked the government set up by the Constitution and that he had suspended Congress. On May 24, 1845, Santa Anna was exiled for life. Canalizo and the four ministers were exiled for ten years. Bancroft, *op cit.*, V, 279.

CHAPTER EIGHT

The United States Invades Mexico—My Return and Final Campaign (1845–1848)

[1] Bancroft gives the date as June 3, 1845. Bancroft, *op. cit.*, V, 280.

[2] It is interesting to note here that Santa Anna appears to have given up any idea of claiming Texas by this time, and refers to the United States' desires for the California, Arizona, and New Mexico areas. Santa Anna fails to mention in his *Memoirs* his many conflicts with the Texans, including the fateful Mier expedition. President Mirabeau B. Lamar of Texas sent an expedition of some 270 volunteer soldiers and about fifty traders from Austin in 1840 to carry the flag of Texas to New Mexico with the idea of asking them to join the Republic. The Mexicans captured the entire expedition and sent them to Mexico City. The Mexicans sent a retaliatory force into Texas in 1842. This force went only as far as San Antonio, but brought back prisoners. The raids continued, until three hundred Texans crossed into Mexico and attacked the town of Mier. They were captured, managed to escape, and then were captured again. A jar was filled with beans, each tenth one being a black one. Each of the prisoners drew a bean, and each man who drew a black one was shot. The others were sent to prison. Wharton, *op. cit.*, 99–100.

[3] On March 8, 1846, Taylor marched from Corpus Christi, arriving on

the Rio Grande on the 28th. He began construction of a fort opposite Matamoras. On April 12, General Ampudia demanded that he withdraw from "Mexican territory," to the northern side of the Nueces. Taylor refused, and General Manuel Arista crossed the Rio Grande. On May 8, he was met by Taylor and defeated at Palo Alto. The next day he was again defeated at Resaca de la Palma. On the 17th, Arista retired, and the next day Taylor advanced northward into Mexico. Robert Selph Henry, *The Story of the Mexican War*, 399–400.

[4] Paredes had been exiled and General Salas was acting President of Mexico at the time of Taylor's invasion. He sent a commission to Havana to ask Santa Anna to return, and Santa Anna sailed for Vera Cruz on a British steamer on the 12th of August. Bancroft, *op. cit.*, V, 301–02.

[5] Commander David Conner of the United States squadron had orders from his government to allow Santa Anna to pass. The United States consul in Havana, Robert B. Campbell, had called on Santa Anna to try to obtain a promise from Santa Anna that he would favor peace with the United States. Santa Anna hedged by saying that he personally favored peace, but would go along with the wishes of his countrymen. *Ibid.*

[6] Bancroft gives the date as August 16, 1846. *Ibid.*

[7] Santa Anna obviously refers to the ridicule which the people afforded him at the time of the Paredes Revolution. The tomb that held his leg was broken open and the leg dragged through the streets. *Ibid.*, 272–273.

[8] Major Solon Borland, Major John P. Gaines, and Captain Cassius M. Clay with scouting parties of eighty men were attacked by three thousand Mexicans under General J. V. Minon and captured on January 22, 1847. Henry, *op. cit.*, 241.

[9] Santa Anna planned to surprise Taylor at Agua Nueva, but found that Taylor had retreated towards Saltillo. Santa Anna believed that the forces had fled. Bancroft, *op. cit.*, V, 419–20.

[10] La Angostura means "the narrows" and refers to a narrow pass between mountains a short distance from Saltillo. These "narrows" form part of the battlefield of Buena Vista. *Ibid.*, 421.

[11] Both sides claimed a victory at the Battle of Buena Vista. Santa Anna claimed to have nineteen thousand five hundred twenty-five men at the battle, but actually had only about fifteen thousand. The American forces totaled four thousand seven hundred fifty-nine. The Americans suffered a total of seven hundred forty-six casualties: two hundred sixty-seven killed, four hundred fifty-six wounded, and twenty-three missing. Henry estimates the Mexican losses at about five times that number. Taylor was granted a special medal by Congress for his victory at Buena Vista. Santa

Anna announced to his Congress that he had won a great victory there and was granted a medal also. Santa Anna returned to Mexico City with his army, making an end to the war in the North. Henry, *op. cit.*, 247–54.

[12] Vera Cruz surrendered to General Scott on March 29, 1847. Bancroft, *op. cit.*, V, 446.

[13] Historians agree with Scott's account of the battle. Scott's victory here was complete, and he dictated his terms to the Mexicans. Santa Anna, knowing that all was lost, fled. *Ibid.*, V, 458–59.

[14] About ten or eleven miles from Puebla.

[15] Mexicalcingo lies in the valley of Mexico about five miles from the city. *Ibid.*, V, 470.

[16] Padierna or Contreras. *Ibid.*, V, 475.

[17] Bancroft states: "The acquisition of Churubusco was valueless, and the expenditure of time and blood upon it a waste." Scott claims to have lost one hundred thirty-nine men, plus eight hundred seventy-six wounded including seventy-six officers. The Mexicans lost four thousand dead, three thousand captured, including two hundred thirteen officers, according to Scott. Scott claims Churubusco as a victory, but unaccountably turned from the site and gave Santa Anna time to recover. *Ibid.*, V, 484–88.

[18] Santa Anna was pleased that Scott proposed to negotiate, as it placed Scott in the position of begging for an armistice. Santa Anna boasted that he suspended hostilities merely to give himself time to prepare for fresh combats. *Ibid.*, V, 490–91.

[19] Mexico was fighting to gain the Nueces as the boundary between Texas and Mexico.

[20] About one-half mile from Chapultepec.

[21] This was perhaps the bloodiest battle of the war. Out of a force of three thousand five hundred soldiers, the Americans lost seven hundred eighty-seven men. Worth claimed that the Mexicans lost over three thousand. Bancroft, *op. cit.*, V, 504–505.

[22] General Persifor F. Smith, who with Generals John A. Quitman and Franklin Pierce, made up the commissioners for the Armistice.

[23] Gamboa accused Santa Anna of not only being a traitor to Mexico in this war, but also in the war of 1836. Genaro Garcia, *Documentos Ineditos o muy Raros para la Historia de Mexico*, XXIX, 6.

[24] Belen Gate fell on September 13, 1847, and the capital was occupied the next day. Bancroft, *op. cit.*, V, 518–19.

[25] Gamboa attempts to clear Terres of any charge, claiming that Santa Anna left Terres with a force insufficient for any defense. According to

Notes

Gamboa, Terres was absolved of all guilt by a later council of war, and Barcena adds that Santa Anna repaired his injustice by giving Terres a pension and restoring his rank. Bancroft, *op. cit.*, V, 518n. Also, "Impugnacion al informe del Exno. Sr. General D. Antonio Lopez de Santa Anna y Constancias en que se apoyan las ampliaciones de la accusacion del Sr. Diputado D. Ramon Gamboa—15 de Julio de 1849," G. Garcia, *Documentos para la Historia de Mexico*, XXIX, 302–304.

[26] Santa Anna resigned on the 16th of September and appointed Manuel de la Pena y Pena as the authority, with generals Herrera and Alcorta as his associates. Peny y Pena declared this unconstitutional, and assumed the office of Provisional President on the 26th of September, with Luis de la Rosa as his sole minister. Bancroft, *op. cit.*, V, 527.

[27] Bancroft states that the force under Colonel Childs consisted of "500 effective men, well armed but otherwise unprovided, and 1,800 invalids." *Ibid.*, V, 528.

[28] General Joseph Lane. For an account of his actions in Mexico at this time and later, see Albert G. Brackett, *General Lane's Brigade in Central Mexico.* (New York, 1854).

[29] Bancroft states that Santa Anna's late military efforts failed through lack of morale among his troops. Also, Santa Anna made many blunders on the battlefield. However, he had many diplomatic triumphs, was energetic and resourceful, and inspired all around him with his zeal. *Ibid.*, V, 533.

CHAPTER NINE

My Attempted Assassination—I Leave for Jamaica (1848)—My Return to Power (1850–1853)

[1] General Lane and the Texas Ranger leader, Colonel Jack Hays, with six hundred men did chase Santa Anna and plunder his home. President Polk's brother obtained Santa Anna's jewel-encrusted cane for the President. Santa Anna's golden sash was allotted to the State of Texas, an oil portrait of him to Indiana, but Santa Anna's wife's dresses were sent to her by the gallant Lane. Hanighen, *op. cit.*, 244–49.

[2] Rumors floated about that Santa Anna desired to continue the war with the United States from the southern provinces. Also, Santa Anna was threatened with court martial by his enemies. Juarez explained to his Congress that if he had allowed Santa Anna to enter Oaxaca, it would have signaled a revolution which had been brewing for some time. Callcott, *op. cit.*, 273.

[3] The *Treaty of Guadalupe Hidalgo* was truly a humiliating one for the

273

Mexican nation. She lost over half her territory for very little indemnity.

⁴ Santa Anna was escorted with military honors by a company of United States cavalry. He wrote a farewell dated March 24, 1848, which carried a forceful appeal to the Mexicans: "Mexicans! One of the leaders of the Revolution for Independence; the one most passionately devoted to your good name; he who had the glory of offering trophies torn from foreign enemies to the Republic; he who has struggled with them conquering a thousand difficulties; he who has shed his blood in the maintenance of your rights; in short, your most loyal friend, addresses to you his last farewell." Quoted in Callcott, *op. cit.*, 275.

⁵ In the wild and hectic election of 1850, Arista beat out his opponents Almonte and Santa Anna, who had been listed by his friends. Arista was never popular, and revolts soon broke out throughout the nation. The clergy and the wealthy again backed Santa Anna, and Arista was considered far too liberal. Arista resigned, and in the following election, Santa Anna carried the vote. General Alvarez and Lucas Alaman threw their support behind Santa Anna and a strong central government. *Ibid.*, 278–82.

CHAPTER TEN

Revolution—Exile Again (1853–1855)

¹ Lombardini was indeed loyal to Santa Anna. This striking military man took over the Presidency from the weak Ceballos, who had taken the post from Arista. It was generally understood that Lombardini was merely holding the post until Santa Anna could return. He had a decree put through Congress calling for a dictator until order was restored. He also stipulated that such a dictator could be a citizen living outside of Mexico. Only Santa Anna could have filled the bill. Hanighen, *op. cit.*, 261–62.

² Santa Anna obviously refers to Lucas Alaman's *Historia de Mejico.*

³ Bancroft states that, "General Juan Alvarez had been at first among Santa Anna's powerful supporters, but soon became disgusted with the dictatorial regime." Bancroft, *op. cit.*, V, 647.

⁴ The *Plan de Auytla* was drawn up on March 1, 1854. It demanded that the dictatorship be abolished, and that a President *ad interim* be elected by representatives of the various states. *Ibid.*, 659.

⁵ No record of the journalist or his work can be found.

⁶ Bancroft states that ". . . after a fruitless effort to take the fort, Santa Anna beat a retreat. . . . The battle of Peregrino was a notable one, and though Santa Anna escaped utter destruction, his loss of men and supplies

was quite large. The remnants of his force had to make their way through burnt fields, annoyed from all sides, till completely battered and exhausted they reached Chilpancingo early in May. After placing detachments in various towns, Santa Anna returned to Mexico." *Ibid.*, 652.

[7] While Santa Anna was reforming the government, cholera raged throughout the nation, drouth destroyed the crops, trade disappeared, and the people grumbled over higher taxes and the increased army recruitment. Hanighen, *op. cit.*, 277.

[8] Santa Anna was in need of money to refurbish his treasury, and the United States was anxious to obtain a block of territory for the purpose of building a transcontinental railroad. At first, Santa Anna demanded $20,000,000 for the territory, which had little value to Mexico. Callcott, *op. cit.*, 294–95.

[9] Gadsden was strongly pro-liberal and outspoken in his criticism of Santa Anna. He wrote, "This is a Government of *plunder* and *necessity*— we can rely on no other influence, but on an appeal to both—We can afford to be liberal in our offers to the first—but the acceptance all depends on our not losing sight of the last—As sensitive as the *Supreme Government* is to Castilian honor when they affect to believe that it is threatened: they are more or equally yielding to a demand which is backed by the power to execute . . . The President though absolute has no head to pursue or maintain a policy—He is as uncertain as the winds and currents which distract him—To maintain his power is his sole end and aim." Quoted in Callcott, *op. cit.*, 295–96.

[10] Gadsden advised that troops be sent to fortify the Rio Grande and that an ample naval force line the Mexican coasts. *Ibid.*

[11] The Gadsden Purchase, which constituted 45,000 square miles of the Mesilla Valley, was obtained for ten million dollars. The Southern Pacific Railroad extended the southern line of New Mexico and Arizona to complete their railroad across the American desert. Wharton, *op. cit.*, 188.

[12] The majority of voters did not vote out of fear, and only the supporters of the government voted to retain Santa Anna in charge of the government. Books were opened at each voting place, and each voter had to fix his signature to his vote. The results showed 400,000 ayes, and very few nays. Bancroft, *op. cit.*, V, 655.

[13] Santa Anna obviously has this vote mixed up with the decree of December 16, 1853, in which he prolonged the dictatorship and awarded himself the title of "Most Serene Highness." In the same decree, he refused the title of "Captain General" and also an increase in pay of $60,000. *Ibid.*, 642–43.

[14] The revolution was gaining momentum throughout the nation. He selected a triumvirate to take charge of the nation, leaving their names in a sealed envelope to be opened when he had departed. Santa Anna issued a proclamation saying that his government had failed because of rebellion. He gladly resigned in order for peace and prosperity to reign. Callcott, *op. cit.*, 314.

CHAPTER ELEVEN

My Exile—Juarez's Rise to Power (1855–1859)

[1] Santa Anna had left the authority for the government in the hands of a triumvirate—Pavon, the President of the Supreme Court, and Generals Salas and Carrera. The triumvirate appointed General Romulo Diaz de la Vega as President *ad interim*. Carrera succeeded him, but resigned shortly thereafter. De la Vega again became President, and was succeeded by General Alvarez in November, 1855. Noll, *op. cit.*, 178–81.

[2] Santa Anna's estates were confiscated by Governor La Llave of Vera Cruz, representing the liberal party in 1855. Presidents Zuloaga and Miramon restored them, along with his military rank. However, on the 6th of July, 1866, he was proclaimed a traitor for his acceptance of the Empire, and his property again confiscated. Bancroft, *op. cit.*, V, 659n.

[3] Comonfort represented the upper class of society, while Alvarez represented the radical liberal wing. Alvarez was evidently unfit for office, and reactionary brutality and intrigues prevailed. Alvarez favored Comonfort, when he realized the popular opinion, and he called a meeting of the liberal party to name his successor. *Ibid.*, 666–72.

[4] A decree was passed on January 9, 1856, stating that Santa Anna, his ministers, and his governors, were responsible for their illegal acts, both to the nation and to individuals. *Ibid.*, 682.

[5] Both the army and the clergy opposed Comonfort. Also, the Treasury had been depleted, as Congress had removed all the taxes set up by Santa Anna. Comonfort and his Congress never agreed, and the radicals accused Comonfort of suppressing reforms. Comonfort tried to unite parties bitterly opposing one another and failed. Even in exile, he tried to serve his country and made attempts to return and defend the liberal principals he believed in. *Ibid.*, 666–729.

[6] Zuloaga and Miramon represented the reactionaries, who with the conservatories and clericals, opposed the Constitution of 1857. Noll, *op. cit.*, 201–229.

[7] Benito Juarez rose from the lowest class of Mexican society to be "one of his country's brilliant lights, statesman, patriot, and representative of a

276

progressive age." An Indian of Oaxaca, Juarez could neither read nor write until the age of twelve. He studied for the clergy before entering the legal profession, obtaining his education from a worthy and charitable citizen. He was a member of the Presidential Cabinet under Alvarez and Governor of Oaxaca. Juarez rose to the head of the Constitutionalists, and his government was recognized by the United States in 1859. He finally defeated Miramon and became President in 1861. Bancroft, *op. cit.*, V, 736–95.

CHAPTER TWELVE

Revolution—The French Empire in Mexico (1859–1865)

[1] An Englishman, Edward Gibbon Swann, added to the legends about Santa Anna by writing a book called *Santa Anna's Ghost*. According to this rather lurid account, Santa Anna could find no peace and tranquility in St. Thomas because of a crime of passion. Santa Anna had supposedly become enamored of a young girl at the time of his defense of the Mexican capital against the Americans. The young lady, Dona Juanita de Islas y Bustamente, in turn loved a young officer, Don Baldomero Valdespina, who supported Santa Anna's enemy, Valencia. When Santa Anna discovered the lovers, he supposedly drew his pistol and shot both the girl and her lover.

Santa Anna's secretary joined a plot by which a Dona Manuela, in love with Santa Anna, impersonated the dead girl by coming to Santa Anna's room during the night, while he was in St. Thomas. When the plot was revealed, Dona Manuela revealed that the girl had not died, but was happily married in Mexico. See Hanighen, *op. cit.*, 288–289. Also, Callcott, *op. cit.*, 324.

[2] Santa Anna had begun negotiations with European courts as early as 1854, using Lucas Alaman, a monarchist, as an intermediary. Possibly he was looking merely for European support against American aggression, but Santa Anna's agent, J. M. Gutierrez de Estrada, continued to press his suit with Queen Isabella in Spain. When Mexico could no longer pay her foreign debts in June, 1861, Napoleon III took advantage of the situation and got in touch with Mexican exiles, who had hoped for a European prince to lead them back to the old days of peace and plenty. Hidalgo and Almonte were among the exiles who fought against Santa Anna's being part of the Empire. Santa Anna wrote to Estrada that Mexico "could not have peace without a radical cure and that cure must be the substitution of a constitutional emperor for that farce called a Republic." Quoted in Callcott, *op. cit.*, 303, 326–27. Also, Bancroft, *op. cit.*, VI, 90–100.

277

[3] Archduke Ferdinand Maximilian of Hapsburg was known as Fernando Maximiliano in Mexico. He was the son of Archduke Franz Karl of Austria and brother of Franz Joseph, the Austrian Emperor. He was married to the daughter of King Leopold I of Belgium. His wife, Marie Charlotte Amelie, was known as Carlota to the Mexicans. Although the Mexican people never desired a monarchy, they greeted the couple with a popular ovation. Maximilian was known for his liberal ideas and innovations while ruling part of the Lombardo-Venetian kingdom. Bancroft, *op. cit.*, VI, 88–89.

[4] Estrada had urged Santa Anna to go to Mexico to lead the movement for Maximilian. But Santa Anna was wise enough to know that the eight thousand soldiers that would accompany Maximilian were enough, and he stalled. Meanwhile, Almonte was fighting against him, and he, himself, accompanied Maximilian. Almonte, Archbishop Labastida, and General Mariano Salas were announced as the members of the Regency. Santa Anna did, however, write to Maximilian on December 22, 1863, stating, "May Your Most Illustrious Highness recognize in the Dean of the Mexican Army a supporter and disinterested friend, and your most obedient servant who wishes you the greatest happiness and who attentively kisses the illustrious hands of Your Most Illustrious Highness." Quoted in Callcott, *op. cit.*, 329–30.

[5] Maximilian's Empire was upheld by French troops. Seeing further examples of French colonization, England and Spain withdrew from Mexico in 1862. Although the United States set a policy of neutrality toward Maximilian's government, it seemed to feel that the Empire lacked stability. Bancroft, *op. cit.*, VI, 99–100.

[6] Santa Anna signed a document recognizing the Intervention and the Empire. He pledged that he would publish no manifestos of political significance and was allowed to proceed toward Mexico City. However, in Orizaba a proclamation was published over his signature which stated that Santa Anna had originally led the movement for democracy, "But the illusions of youth are passed and in the presence of the great disasters brought about by the system (democracy), I do not wish to deceive anyone; the last word of my conscience and of my convictions, is a constitutional monarchy." Santa Anna insisted that he knew nothing of the document and that his friends had published it, but the French ordered him to leave the country. Quoted in Callcott, *op. cit.*, 331. Also, Bancroft, *op. cit.*, V, 658n.

[7] Maximilian might have profited from Santa Anna's advice. Santa Anna wrote to a friend during Maximilian's reign, "If I could have talked to the

Emperor, as I desired, I would have told him without beating about the bush: that he should adopt the religious principle as the basis for his throne, the support of the conservatives and landlords, together with that of the Clergy and Army, uniting in the latter the old veterans and the best youth of the country. But the events of the 12th of March (the expulsion from Vera Cruz) which you witnessed, separated me from the Monarch, and my noble desires were frustrated." Quoted in Callcott, *op. cit.*, 332.

[8] This *Manifesto* read, "LIBERALS AND CONSERVATIVES! Let us forget our fraticidal contests and go forward! Let us unite against the common enemy. One single flag covers us, the flag of liberty; one single thought animates us, that of war to the death against the invaders who destroy our towns and kill our brothers. Eternal hatred to the tyrants of our Native Land!

"Fellow citizens! On the memorable 2nd of December, 1822, I took as a motto these words: *Down with the Empire! Long Live the Republic!* Now from the foreign soil on which I find myself, I repeat it with the same enthusiasm." Quoted in Callcott, *op. cit.*, 335.

CHAPTER THIRTEEN

Mr. Seward—The Infamous Plot Against Me (1865–1866)

[1] William H. Seward was Secretary of State under Andrew Johnson. He came to the West Indies supposedly for his health, but actually to look over the prospects for signing a treaty with Denmark for the purchase of the Danish West Indies, among which was St. Thomas. Seward arrived in the harbor on the United States Man-of-War *Desoto,* and he called on Santa Anna merely as a social call. Frederick Bancroft, *The Life of William H. Seward,* 481–82.

[2] General Jose A. Paez was a distinguished Venezuelan patriot and Minister to the United States in 1861. When his political party, the Centralists, were defeated in 1863, he moved to New York.

CHAPTER FOURTEEN

My Trip to New York—Further Infamies (1866–1867)

[1] The *New York Herald* published a proclamation sent out by Santa Anna, and the press gave Santa Anna's arrival quite a play. However, no representatives of the State Department received him, and the Mexican Minister publicly denounced him. The Mexican Club of New York published a denunciation of him, citing his career. Callcott, *op. cit.*, 340–41.

[2] Santa Anna hired an English interpreter and secretary, James Adams, who lived in Elizabeth Port. Adams noticed Santa Anna chewing pieces

of a tropical vegetable, and he inquired what it was. Santa Anna told him it was chicle, and left the young man with the remainder when he left the United States, Adams mixed the chicle with sweetening elements and placed it on the market. Santa Anna's gift formed the basis of the new and lucrative industry, the famous Adams Chewing Gum Company. Hanighen, *op. cit.*, 298.

[3] Santa Anna's nephew suspected that his uncle was the victim of a plot and wrote to Seward asking him if he had entered into a treaty to support his uncle. In reply, Seward stated plainly, ". . . this government has not recognized any other Mexican authority, or held correspondence, or entered into negotiations, with any other than that of President Don Benito Juarez." Quoted in Callcott, *op. cit.*, 342.

CHAPTER FIFTEEN

Back to Vera Cruz—Imprisonment (1867)

[1] Callcott gives this date as March 22, with Santa Anna reaching Vera Cruz on June 3. After he had set sail from New York, the city of Tamaulipas recognized Santa Anna as head of the Mexican armies and as President *ad interim* of Mexico. It would seem that Santa Anna's plan was to seize Vera Cruz and set up a Conservative government to defeat Juarez' radical government. Callcott, *op. cit.*, 344.

[2] After trying to convince the officers of the garrison at Vera Cruz that a Republic was necessary, Santa Anna met with many refusals. Many of the officers were still loyal to the Empire, and others were disgusted with Santa Anna's leaving Mexico." Hanighen, *op. cit.*, 300.

[3] The United States Consul E. H. Saulnier felt that Santa Anna could not have the support of the United States government and ordered Commander F. A. Roe of the *Tacony* to prevent Santa Anna from landing. Santa Anna was allowed to depart on the *Virginia* with the understanding that he not return to Vera Cruz. Callcott, *op. cit.*, 345–46.

[4] Santa Anna delivered a proclamation here, stating, "Yucatecans! Finding myself so near to you on my way to the paternal soil, I hasten to salute you, profoundly moved on contemplating the immense contrast between what we were and what we are today. You remember that in the years 1824 and 1825 I had the honor of exercising in this Peninsula the highest military and political authority and that I received friendly demonstrations from you which I could not forget . . . My mission among you is purely of peace and concord. In critical times I come to offer my helpful mediation, among the disharmonious members of the family." Quoted in Hanighen, *op. cit.*, 301–02.

[5] Captain John Deaken of the *Virginia* protested that Commander Roe had instructed him to see that Santa Anna did not land on Mexican soil. Callcott, *op. cit.*, 347.

[6] Seward received many protests that the American flag had been flaunted, and New York papers published the news that Santa Anna had been executed, as well as Maximilian. The New York *Express* printed an editorial, stating, "The worst fears of the friends of Santa Anna have finally been realized. The same fate which befell the unfortunate Prince Maximilian a few weeks ago has also overtaken the ex-dictator. In truth it appears that the mestizo, creole [sic] Indian Benito Juarez is of the same mould as those who do not hold the least sample in 'dirtying themselves to gain a throne,' closing the doors of mercy to humanity. He could have done better to pardon Santa Anna, letting the poor old man return as a proof that even a Mexican President is not a monster of cruelty as has generally been believed in view of the assassination of Prince Maximilian." Quoted in Hanighen, *op. cit.*, 303.

CHAPTER SIXTEEN
My Trial (1867)

[1] Condemning Santa Anna to exile instead of to death was probably a very wise move, as the United States was none too pleased over Santa Anna's being removed from a ship flying the American flag. Callcott, *op. cit.*, 349–50.

[2] The prosecuting attorney did indeed ask the death penalty, but Santa Anna's defending attorney arose with the words, "Crucify him! Crucify him! thus shouted the Jewish rabble." His defense of Santa Anna was an impassioned and brilliant one. *Ibid.*

CHAPTER SEVENTEEN
The Plottings of Juarez—My Last Journey to Nassau (1867–1872)

[1] Santa Anna probably refers to an appeal he made to Seward to which Seward replied that the United States was not in sympathy with Santa Anna and stating that the United States was in accord with the government of Juarez. Callcott, *op. cit.*, 341.

Bibliography

Bibliography

Books

Allesio Robles, Vito. *Coahuila y Texas.* Mexico: Talles Grafios de la Nacion, 1945–46.

Bancroft, Frederick. *The Life of William H. Seward.* New York and London: 1919.

Bancroft, Hubert Howe. *History of the Pacific States of North America: History of Mexico.* San Francisco: A. L. Bancroft & Company, Publishers, 1883–1888.

Bancroft, Hubert Howe. *History of the Pacific States of North America: Texas.* San Francisco: A. L. Bancroft & Company, Publishers, 1889.

Brackett, Albert G. *General Lane's Brigade in Central Mexico.* New York: 1854.

Callcott, Wilfrid Hardy. *Santa Anna: The Story of an Enigma Who Once Was Mexico.* Norman: University of Oklahoma Press, 1936.

Carroll, H. Bailey, Frances Nesmith, and Mary Jane Gentry. *The Story of Texas.* New York: Noble and Noble, Publishers, Inc., 1963.

Castaneda, Carlos E. (trans.). *The Mexican Side of the Texan Revolution.* Dallas: L. P. Turner Company, Publishers, 1928.

Cotner, Thomas E., and Carlos E. Castaneda (eds.). *Essays in Mexican History.* Austin: The Institute of Latin American Studies, The University of Texas, 1958.

Dixon, Sam Houston, and L. W. Kemp. *The Heroes of San Jacinto.* Houston: Anson Jones Press, 1932.

Edwards, John N. *Shelby's Expedition to Mexico: An Unwritten Leaf of the War.* Austin: The Steck Company, Publishers, 1964.

Fisher, Howard T., and Marion Hall (eds.). *Life in Mexico: The Letters of Fanny Calderon de la Barca.* New York: Doubleday and Company, Inc., 1966.

Hanighen, Frank C. *Santa Anna: The Napoleon of the West.* New York: Coward-McCann, Inc., 1934.

Henry, Robert Selph. *The Story of the Mexican War.* New York: 1952.

Hollon, W. Eugene, and Ruth Lapham Butler (eds.). *William Bollaert's Texas.* Norman: University of Oklahoma Press, 1956.

James, Marquis. *The Raven: A Biography of Sam Houston.* Indianapolis: The Bobbs-Merrill Company, 1929.

Newell, Chester. *History of the Revolution in Texas.* Austin: The Steck Company, Publishers, 1935.

285

Bibliography

Noll, Arthur H. *From Empire to Republic*. Chicago: A. C. McClurg and Company, 1903.

Noll, Arthur H. *A Short History of Mexico*. Chicago: A. C. McClurg and Company, 1905.

Raines, C. W. *A Bibliography of Texas*. Austin: The Gammel Book Co., 1896.

Smith, Justin. *The War with Mexico*. New York: Macmillan Company, 1919.

Smithwick, Noah. *The Evolution of a State or Recollections of Old Texas Days*. (Compiled by his daughter Nanna Smithwick Donaldson.) Austin: 1900.

Steen, Ralph W. *History of Texas*. Austin: The Steck Company, Publishers, 1939.

Streeter, Thomas W. *Bibliography of Texas*. Harvard University Press, 1960.

Wallace, Ernst, and David M. Vignes. *Documents of Texas History*. Austin: The Steck Company, Publishers, 1963.

Webb, Walter Prescott, and H. Bailey Carroll (eds.). *The Handbook of Texas*. Austin: The Texas State Historical Association, 1952.

Wharton, Clarence R. *El Presidente: A Sketch of the Life of General Santa Anna*. Austin: Gammel's Book Store, 1926.

Wooten, Dudley G. (ed.). *A Comprehensive History of Texas*. Dallas: William G. Scharff, 1898.

Yoakum, Henderson. *History of Texas, from Its First Settlement in 1765 to Its Annexation to the United States in 1846*. New York: J. S. Redfield, 1855.

Theses, Manuscripts, Documents, Pamphlets, Articles

"Autograph of the Quarter," *Manuscripts*, XIV, No. 3 (Summer, 1962).

The Battle of San Jacinto. Houston: Union National Bank, 1936.

Davenport, Harbert. "Men of Goliad," *Southwestern Historical Quarterly*, XLIII.

East, Ernest E., "Santa Anna's Cork Leg," *Illinois Archival Information* (April, 1954).

Filisola, Vicente. *Memorias para la Historia de la Guerra de Tejas*. (Mexico City: 1848).

Filisola, Vicente. *Representacion Dirigida al Supremo Gobierno por el General Vicente Filisola, en Defensa de Su Honor y Aclaracion de Sus Operaciones como General en Gefe del Ejercito sobre Tejas*. (Mexico City: 1836).

286

Bibliography

Garcia, Genero. *Documentos Ineditos o muy Raros para la Historia de Mexico*, XXIX.

Harris, Helen W. The Public Life of Juan Nepomuceno Almonte. (Unpublished Ph.D. Thesis, The University of Texas, 1935).

Jackson, Andrew. *Message from the President . . . Transmitting His Correspondence with General Santa Anna. . . .* (Washington, January 18, 1837).

Raines, C. W. "Life of Antonio Lopez de Santa Anna," *Texas Magazine*, I.

Urrea, Jose, *Diario de las Operaciones Militares . . . en la Campana de Tejas*. Victoria de Durango: 1838.

Williams, Amelia. "A Critical Study of the Siege of the Alamo and of the Personnel of its Defenders," *Southwestern Historical Quarterly*, XXXVII.

Winkler, E. W. "The 'Twin Sisters' Cannon, 1836–1865," *Southwestern Historical Quarterly*, XXI.

287

Index

Index

291

Index

Index

293

Index

294

Index

295

Index